AF615499

LECTURES ON LOGIC BY FRITZ MEDICUS

Translation by
Fritz Marti
Commentary by
Fritz Marti and Heinrich A. Medicus

UNIVERSITY
PRESS OF
AMERICA

Copyright © 1982 by
University Press of America, Inc.™
P.O. Box 19101, Washington, D.C. 20036

All rights reserved

Printed in the United States of America

ISBN: 0-8191-2114-2 (Perfect)

Library of Congress Number: 81-40825

TABLE OF CONTENTS

The Lectures

Apparatus

Preface

From 1911 till his retirement in 1946, Fritz Medicus was professor of philosophy and pedagogy at the Sxiss Federal Institute of Technology in Zürich. It was known from its foundation in 1955 as the Eidgenössische (i.e. federal) Polytechnikum but renamed in 1911 Eidgenössische Technische Hochschule, or ETH for short.

When Medicus died in 1956, his papers were given to the library of the ETH. This Medicus Archive was now to be catalogued and enlarged by items of correspondence and by student notes taken in the courses given by Medicus. Early this year, I sent to the ETH Library photostats of my notes taken 1915-20. As I browsed in them, I found the Logic of 1919 especially alive. Much of it may strike today's readers as new. I feel it should not be kept hidden in an archive.

Medicus was a brilliant and fast lecturer. Even a stenographer would have felt rushed. What I learned to do during my four or five years in Medicus' classroom was to take down outstanding sentences as literally as I could. I am surprised to find my string of key sentences quite coherent, with seldom any gap in thought. However the translation of my notes presented two difficulties. The greater philosophical flexibility of German often demands that an original sentence be rendered by more than one sentence in English. Furthermore, Medicus' very sensitive use of words and many innovations in terminology often require an interpretative translation. Thus the notes taken in my youth had now to be recast three scores of years later. Still I dare say I am here presenting the very essence of what Medicus had to say in the summer of 1919.

Since then, the physical sciences have made tremendous strides. The large audiences of Medicus consisted mainly of students of engineering and natural science. His illustrations borrowed from these sciences were of course dated. This requires an occasional explanation of the status of physics at that time, and I am happy to have the physicist son of Medicus as my collaborator in writing the necessary commentary.

South Bend, Indiana, August 1981. Fritz Marti

INTRODUCTORY INFORMATION

On style:

Medicus never handed out written guidelines for his courses. It was not customary. It is often done in America, and students find it helpful. Nor did Medicus always explicitly announce a new chapter or section of his lectures. He left such bookkeeping to his hearers. I have done it in this book by means of two devices. I have inserted the chapter headings which also furnish my table of contents. And I have abstracted what I am calling the plan of the lectures.

Readers who are not allergic to German may appreciate my not infrequent parentheses in which I put German phrases for which I have no entirely plain English equivalent.

On terms:

Medicus was fond of stressing the life of truth. Truths do not lie around like pebbles or shells on the beach, although there are always lots of truths not yet discovered by man. Pebbles may be polished and shells broken by the waves. Thus they change passively. But every truth is an active challenge to the mind. As the mind discovers it, the truth receives an historical formulation. Yet the words which voice it can neither shackle nor kill it. The truth itself demands a reformulation in the next mind. It is nothing passive, nothing dead.

In the lecture of May 14, Medicus said our "laying claim to truth must be experienced (erlebt) not merely observed." (Page 10). Even before the First World War, German philosophical literature abounded in the words erleben and das Erleben. More recently there is much international talk about "existence." Of course it is an old story. Augustine said nothing is as much in the mind as the mind itself (de Trinitate X, viii, 11). Kant wrote: "in the awareness of myself, in sheer thinking, I am the essence itself" (Critique of Pure Reason 429). And Fichte kept repeating that "as I, I am for myself alone." --If the reader comes to think of it, he will readily grant that nobody can be his I for him. Fichte wrote in 1797, "the first assignment philosophy gives to its pupil is: Heed your own self, turn your attention away from everything around you, look into yourself! That is the first topic, nothing else" (I, 422). --I cannot "observe" my I like a stranger; I can only be my I in sheer awareness. --This also explains the word immediacy Medicus often uses. See the index.

At the end of the lecture of May 14 (page 11) Medicus said: "As soon as the I detaches itself from the [life of the] content of his thought, the latter becomes an object which lacks any inherent relation to truth." It becomes a mere notion in the mind. And notions in the mind are not necessarily true. They may turn out to be false. Yet even such false _representations_ may give the impression of being true. In order to make any sense at all, something in error must be true. If we can spot it, the error disappears. --Naive, logically untutored minds believe truths are like gold or silver coins whose value does not change. These immature minds would like to shirk the human duty to check and recheck. They may throw that duty in the lap of their doctrinaire kind of God "who knows everything" already. If they grew up they would discover with Augustine that God _is_ the living truth that "teaches inwardly", as _summa magistra_ (_de libero arbitrio_ II, xv, 9 and II, ii, 4). --Consult the index on representation (Vorstellung).

What we are looking for when we seek certainty is the _necessity of thought_, the cogency of reason. (In this context, the word "necessity" does not at all mean "need.") --In the lecture of May 19, Medicus explained that "necessity of thought must not and cannot be merely accepted", the way we can and do accept many a contingent thing. We can understand _why_ it is necessary or cogent. (Page 16)

At the beginning of the lecture of May 21, Medicus said "_natural_ necessity connects objects" (page 16). The faculty by which we ascertain the connection is ratiocination (Verstand).--Last spring it was exactly two hundred years since 1781 when the first edition of the _Critique of Pure Reason_ appeared and made explicitly clear the distinction between ratiocination (Verstand) which ascertains what is objective, contingent and conditional, and reason (Vernunft) which seeks the unconditional. --On the European continent, the distinction is the basic intellectual tool of every properly trained academic. This side of the British Channel, there are still academics, even some professional philosophers who share the pre-Kantian and really medieval notion that reason _is_ ratiocination. --This book is not the place to sketch the history of the distinction which goes back to Augustine, Plato, even Parmenides. It should suffice to quote a few sentences of Medicus. In his book of 1951 on _Menschlichkeit_, translated 1973 as _On Being Human_, he wrote about ratiocination or intelligence: "our intelligence is what _we_ have, and each one has his own. But reason has _us_: we are held fast and supported by its superindividual necessity. We _must_ distinguish between true and false" (78). --The reader may want to make use of the index on the two terms, as they are _distinguished_ (_not_ separated) throughout the book.

On page arrangement:

The translation always starts at the left margin. The commentary is indented by ten letter spaces. Where nothing else is said, the comments are mine. The comments by Heinrich Medicus are marked by HM.

Translator's insertions appear in brackets [ ].

In Greek words, ä stands for eta, w for omega.

THE PLAN OF THE LECTURES

The topic of logic is not timeless abstractions but the comprehension of the historical life of truth, in the different disciplines. The goal of logic is an insight into the interrelation of these disciplines, particularly in science.

Psychology investigates observed facts. What is logical, however, is not a matter of mere observation. For psychology "thoughts" are facts, regardless of their truth or falsehood.

Concrete logic (of content) does not seek the abstractions of formal logic, whose so-called "laws of thinking" have validity only in and from concrete contents.

The awareness of the logical subject is impersonal. Therefore it establishes an immediate community of understanding.

A thought's relation to reality is logically primary. To think means to be grasped by the meaning of the specific content of thought.

Every concept grows; it becomes richer owing to every pertinent judgment. Every necessity of thought (or cogency) is certain of and by itself. The interconnection of specific contents of thought is cogently necessary.

Whatever is true knowledge has the form of I, i.e. the certainty of "I am I". Every Not-I confronts the I as an infinite task.

There are kinds and degrees of reality, of existence. The concept and the reality conceived are the same.

We can think sense evidence only by taking it as a representative of a law. Hypotheses do contain truth because they conform to a necessity of thought which operates already in the formulation of a question, in the surmise of a law.

The history of science is the history of always onesided hypotheses. Hypotheses seek "essences", i.e. universal validity, i.e. concepts. Hypotheses are always better than their historically conditioned formulations. An "essence" is the fusion of the specific substance and causality.

The frontier of physics is forever new. --Space and time are one. Mathematical spece comes "late", by reflection, not observation.

Biological science goes beyond physical determination, though it does not deny it. --Thinking is life that knows itself. This fact might furnish a model for biological essences.

Historical reality is still more than biological. The truth of the latter is not unconditional. To grasp that "higher" life is the task of the historical disciplines.

Lectures on Logic

May 5, 1919 INTRODUCTION TO THE PROBLEM OF LOGIC

The naive mythological explanation of our existence needs clarification. It is rectified (geläutert) by philosophy.

> To rectify can mean to distil; and that is what happens, figuratively, when mythological images are no longer taken as a kind of photographs of personages and events. Instead of rectification (which could mean correction of mistakes) we had better say verification. Philosophy is not fault finding. It looks for what is undeniably true (verum) in the mythological message.

Philosophy was shaken up in the fifth century B.C. by Parmenides. He found that not-being is not. A corollary would say there can be no becoming, no transition from not-being to being. Such a transition resists conceptualization. It lacks the necessity of thought. It is not possible to think the world of becoming, the world of nature. Nature is an appearance without essence (wesenloser Schein). What truly is has neither become nor can it pass away.

Zeno, the pupil of Parmenides, gave examples of the impossibility of thinking events in experience. For instance the race between Achilles and the tortoise; or a flying arrow.

> While Achilles covers the distance the tortoise was ahead at the start, the tortoise crawls ahead, and Achilles has to make up that gap. And so ad infinitum. He can never overtake the tortoise. How does the arrow get from one position to the next? To say "it flies" means to beg the question. How are we to think movement?

> At the foot of my note page, I referred to the Galilean relativity of motion. Things move relatively to each other. There is no absolute motion. In completely empty space one can no longer ascertain whether a thing moves or not.

> Of course Medicus threw the Eleatic puzzles at us to make us ask ourselves questions.

The successful mastery of engineering problems can seemingly resolve the logical difficulty only for an unquestioning mind, but that success merely enhances the scruples of the philosopher.

The historical and natural sciences and their professional critiques accept the truth value of their facts without further ado. For philosophy that value is problematic. In that respect philosophy is "theory of knowledge" (Wissenschaftslehre), it is logic.

"In how far are the forms of our thinking able to grasp what is true." (See Hegel's Logic.)

Likewise the philosophy of right and of religion, as well as aesthetics, cannot neglect their logical problems without becoming dogmatic. Philosophy is indispensable for sound living (lebensnotwending). To be sure the majority goes along with their cultural dogmas. Yet those who demand self-reliance differ and want to be among those who bear the weight of the problems.

May 7 Literature: There is no German book for a deeper study of the content of these lectures, except Hegel's Logic which is already far back.

BENEDETTO CROCE: Logica, conoscenza del concetto puro (second volume of the Filosofia, conoscenza dello spirito.)

Stadler's Logik (ed. by Platter, Leipzig 191) is the exact opposite of Medicus.

Introductory are:

Rickert: Die Grenzender naturwissenschaftlichen Begriffsbildung (Heidelberg).

Eucken: Erkennen und Leben (Leipzig 1912).

THE PLACE AND FUNCTION OF LOGIC AMONG THE OTHER DISCIPLINES

Today the coherence of the individual sciences is lost. They cannot even fight with each other when of different opinion. The common scientific ground is lacking.

Every scientist is at least dimly conscious of the oneness of truth. But today this consciousness is no living power.

> When Medicus says "that the truth is one," he is skirting mythological speech. Fulfledged mythology defies The Truth and in so doing it rightly wants to retain the life of the truth and therefore must personify it, for instance in the Christ. Yet, lest such a divine person remain transcendent and beyond reach, the myth must also retain the unexceptional

specificity of truth and therefore must assert the Incarnation. For the Gautama Buddha truth, in the abstract, is "the right path" to be found and trodden by all. The unique specificity of the incarnate Christ is in danger of becoming the all consuming godhead. It appears as a once and for all sum total of truth, therefore lifeless. Therefore the Christian myth must teach, not that God is a person, but that God is a Trinity of three hypostases or persons, and that there is an alive communication between the three (though presumably beyond man's insight).

Of course Medicus is not a mythologist. When he speaks of "the truth" in the singular he means that "living power" which does not at all overpower and enslave us in some orthodoxy but which, instead, liberates us from the threatening shackles that lie in the apparent finality of any one specific truth. Every truth demands being voiced in clear words, and the wording, for the moment, seems final. (Hence the popular belief that there must be a kind of comprehensive encyclopedia or a divine mind that "knows it all.")

"The truth is one" means that every specific truth wants to be in line with every other and therefore cannot have its own final form. Formulations must be clear and adequate but can never be final. For truth is indeed what Medicus calls a "living power." It is liberating not confining. It is communicable and communicative and thus can properly be called one. (Mythology says the same thing when, with Paul, it exclaims, "though crucified with Christ, nevertheless I live, yet not I, but Christ lives in me." Gal. 2:20) It is the life of truth that lets us live <u>in</u> our seeking and finding. And it is all pervasive, never bottled up in an individual, with the effect of possessing the individual rather than being its possession. Truth makes free. (The mythological Christ is <u>soter</u>, savior, liberator.)

Theology and natural science are in contact only through philosophy, above all in logic.

After all, we should like to know in what way each domain of reason contributes to scientific culture which by no means is a mere abstraction. In the discipline of <u>logic</u> the <u>scientific life</u> gives itself an account of what it is and desires. In the individual sciences reason ceases to be a mere abstraction. At the same time each individual science also desires to recognize its own significance. Logic is the self-recognition of reason, in regard to the theoretic aspect of reason.

> Reason also lives "practically", that is, in problems what to do, and likewise aesthetically, e.g. seeking the right words.

The goal of logic is to gain insight into the interdependence of the different determinations of reason. As a lecturer and teacher I cannot lead you to that goal because reason is nothing static like an Indian god in his manifold shapes. Reason is life which has no end. Scientific culture never speaks its final word. Perhaps a final word can be spoken about the culture of a people. But reason itself goes on. Science (Wissenschaft) has a boundless history.

> HM In German, "Wissenschaft" encompasses not only the natural sciences and mathematics, but also the social sciences and humanities; the latter are called "Geisteswissenschaften", as contrasted to "Naturwissenschaft." We may say that "Wissenschaft" encompasses all scholarly endeavors.

To be sure there was a prevailing opinion that logic must be timeless because "truth does not change." Yet the question regarding "laws of reason" has its root in the question regarding the essence or nature (das Wesen) of truth.

There is a history of science. Thus we shall not consult Aristotle (whose greatness we do not question) when we desire to know the logical structure of modern scientific labor, for instance the theory of relativity.

What we seek is the unity among the many meanings of science in the awareness of our culture, regardless of the existence of that awareness in any one man. That existence might be postulated in "the scientist as such."

Only in as far as we see that unity can we recognize the place of our own chosen discipline. The system of disciplines is alive. The individual sciences grow and with them the whole. However the different sciences do not grow at the same rate of speed. Thus the center of gravity shifts in the system of the sciences. Yet neither the individual sciences nor their whole grow by themselves. Logic must grow, so that the sciences do not lose themselves.

Logic needs the sciences in the same way in which aesthetics needs the arts. The first task of logic is not any endeavor to complete its own past.

> This is an abvious side thrust of Medicus at our century's cultivation of logic _in vetro_, cultivating aloof abstractions.

The first task of logic is to gain insight into the structure of contemporary science. The logician must size up the sciences, measuring them against the consciousness of culture. Thus for instance zoology obtained a new place in culture owing to the work of Lamark and Darwin. Another example: What today's zoology calls an atavism, was formerly taken to be something new in the making.

May 12

To find one's place in the whole contemporary culture is the task of philosophical education; logical education has the same task with regard to the whole of science. To be sure, no individual can absorb the whole of culture. The individual is only a member, yet he can at least be an independent member.

FORMAL LOGIC

Formalistic logic is a dubious heirloom of late antiquity and of the middle ages. It ignores the historical conditions of all science. It is true that the older systems of metaphysics lacked the historical point of view. Nevertheless it is not as false to say the world remains unchanged, than to say the same of science.

Formal syllogistics is mostly a dreary and sterile abstraction.

Logic does not teach to think. True, nobody claims it does. Yet one does expect logic to check the correctness of what is being thought. However that is not the question. The correctness of abstract formulae must first be tested by means of concrete examples. The logical "rules" are not self-evident. For instance there is a rule that says: "If one converts a general judgment, it turns into a particular." This rule can be understood only by looking at a concrete example.

> In 1923 my first assignment at the University of Oregon was a course in formal logic. Having just arrived from Europe, I naively assumed that any student accepted for university study had to have a thorough background in grammar and mathematics and therefore did not need to "learn to think." I had the textbook and found it very boring. So I went before my class and told the youngsters that all we could hope to accomplish in this class was a kind of balance sheet of what had been practiced

for years in high school. (I still believed that high schools prepare for college.) So, I said: You have browsed in this textbook and discovered such terms as syllogism. What is a syllogism? Let us take an example. Do you grant that all dogs are mammals?--Heads nodded.--Well then, assume that you know nothing at all except that all dogs are mammals. What can you safely say about mammals?--The eager hopeful in the front row shot up his hand and asserted: All mammals are dogs.--Many faces expressed doubt. On my part I realized that these kids did need the skill "how to think." We then looked at the book and found the rule that a judgment of the form A does not convert to A but only to I. Only <u>some</u> mammals are dogs. What kind of judgment does convert to its own form. E! For example: "No whale is a fish" converts to "no fish is a whale." But the validity of the rule lies in the examples, not vice versa.

Fichte spoke of "<u>real</u> thinking." Logic can be fertile only if it helps the scientist ascertain his place in the whole of his science. It is sterile if it undertakes to check the validity of the scientist's scientific thoughts.

The logician had better learn how to think scientifically before he makes bold to help the scientist in his orientation in the whole. It is the scientist, not the logician, who furthers science.

Abstract formal logic cannot even grasp the meaning of revolutions in science. And in science revolutions are always good. In order that logical rules can be set up, the <u>living</u> awareness of truth must already be present. At best--if the scientist is at the same time philosophical--logic may discover a new thought simultaneously with concrete science.

HM In 1919, Medicus had an eminent scientific colleague and friend at the Institute, the mathematical physicist Hermann Weyl. Among this scholar's main research interests, at that time, was the general theory of relativity and the unified field theory. For about half a year, 1913-14, Weyl and Einstein were colleagues at the Swiss Federal Institute of Technology. In the 1930's, Weyl became again a colleague of Einstein at the Institute for Advanced Study in Princeton. -- [I well remember how Weyl and his wife diligently attended many a lecture course of Medicus.--F. Marti.]

Fichte said: "The only undertaking that is its own end is the life of the mind. There can be no other." (VII,55)

> Fichte used the phrase "das geistige Leben." It is very questionable to translate Geist as spirit. Spirit is not only too vague a word, but many English speakers use it as if it pointed at a distant, even unknowable entity. And "spiritually" often means something "out of this world." Our "mind" at least is supposed to be present, even if we are absent-minded. On the other hand, "mind" is identical with the individual's mental events. There is no mass mind. But "geistiges Leven" unites us, just because it is an undertaking of responsibility which occurs only by autonomous act. When we are most ourselves then we are most open to all who are of good will. The Greek word nous may come closest to Geist. But Greek is quite out of fashion. The Hellenistic word pneuma, like the English spirit is not unambiguous. As I translate the next sentence of Medicus I find myself bound to use the noun spirit or the mawkish adjective spiritual. May the reader cleanse it from every trace of mawkishness.

If logic is to make clear the mental contexts, it must subordinate itself to the life of the spirit (the spiritual life).

> The self-subordination is necessary because the life of the truth is not merely logical but also moral. Its very root is aesthetic. (About that more later.)

May 14 LOGIC AND PSYCHOLOGY

One must distinguish between merely possible and necessary relations of the contents of thought.

It seems as if the psychology of knowing had the same object as logic. Psychology analyses our representations (Vorstellungen).

> The English word "representation" is not as automatically selfexplanatory as the German "Vorstellung". -- If I find the little bottle of Liquid Paper lying on my desk I must stand (stellen) it up. It then stands in front (vor) of me as an object, when I am awake. But likewise it stands before my mind when I am dreaming it. The latter Vorstellung could quite properly be called a re-presentation, representing or presenting again what formerly had been present as a physical object. Of course when physically present,

that physical presence had to be transposed into the mental presence. Thus it also became a re-presentation. The English word has the advantage of covering non-visual presences as well as visual. Hence its "abstractness" and apparent lack of self-explanation. On the other hand, in German our dreams are "blosse Vorstellungen", mere mental presences, not physical. -- Psychology deals with both kind of representations, for they are both "in the mind."

Psychology analyzes them, studies their sequel as a process under natural law, and calls the process thinking. At least this is what psychology did in the nineteenth century. Nowadays we know that thinking is no mere movement of representations, because such thoughts as "validity" claim a relation to truth.

As a natural science psychology must ignore this relation. It does not ask whether our representations are true, but merely whether or not they are facts found in some individual mind. -- Truth is the implicit concern of every sound mind, whether or not the individual knows it explicitly. -- I as I seek truth. So do you. If we abstract from this quest, we call the natural sequel of representations truth. Then:

The old psychological explanation of "thinking", which abstracts from the search for truth winds up without an I. As Hume correctly pointed out, for that explanation the I is only "a bundle of perceptions". And the I or self passively suffered the sequel of its representations.

Modern psychology of thought acknowledges the thinking I as creative. Nevertheless the distinction between psychology and logic holds. The psychology of thinking needs to borrow logical insights, while the psychology of mere associations was in no such need.

In its method <u>psychology</u> is a natural science. Its laws operate unconsciously, just like mechanical and physiological laws. <u>Logic</u> however inquires into laws of selfcertain awareness. To be sure, the distinction between the two disciplines is no longer so sharp and obvious. In books of modern psychology of thinking there are passages which could as well be found in a book on logic, passages which are actually borrowed from the discipline of logic.

It was Husserl who gave the impetus for a psychology of thinking. And Husserl was significant in logic. -- As an example we find Ebbinghaus saying that insights into truths as well as errors result from the same laws.

> In 1897 Ebbinghaus (1850-1909) published his Grundzüge der Psychologie, still a favorite psychology text in 1919. -- Edmund Husserl, born 1859, since 1916 taught at the University of Freiburg in Breisgau. He is well known as the founder of modern Phenomenology and, in 1913, the founder of the Yearbook for Philosophy and Phenomenological Research.

There is in us a drive for intellectual self-assertion. Thus three year old children always ask for the name of things. To identify the name means to ascertain a truth.

> (My notes have my Nietzschean remark: Truth as will for power over the flux of appearances. That is also a psychologism.)

To inquire into the thinking of the three year olds is not the task of the logician but of the psychologist who, however, needs logical schooling in order to be able to recognize the logical needs.

Not only logical but also ethical categories enter into the discussion. Thus, for instance, one often does not want to see certain things as they are.

> The newspapers bring daily examples. We Americans do not want to see that the Soviet regime is state capitalism, not communism. We do not want to see that Marxism is a religion, in fact a mid-nineteen century atheistic version of early Christianity. -- The Reader's Digest of April 1981 asks us to see the plight of the Afghans fighting their holy war against the Russian invasion. That we see readily. But when it comes to seeing San Salvador in its complexity, we quickly paste the poster COMMUNISM over the sore spot, trying to dodge the moral question.

The focus of logic is fixed on those necessities of thought which seek a victory over such weaknesses as not wanting to see what is. This quest is what psychology must acknowledge as a human trait. However psychology can never hope to explain the aim of truth psychologically. In contrast, zoology can hope to recognize the formation of a specific species of animals.

Psychology investigates facts. It deals with what can be observed. What is logical is never a matter of mere observation Validity or laying claim to truth must be experienced (erlebt) not merely observed.

> It is the plight of present day education that the schools have failed to make pupils see the difference between mere individual observation and personal experience of superindividual validity. -- In the 1920's, a physicist colleague of mine asked me quite seriously: "How can you know that 2 and 2 are 4?" I replied: "By adding them up!" But his lack of logical schooling made him cling to his skepsis. Nowadays the young seem to clutch the same so-called philosophy. The result is a basic hopeless loneliness.

Self-certainty can be experienced (erlebt) only in immediacy.

> Without any apparent knowledge of Augustine, it was Kant who brought into focus this immediacy, and his followers, Fichte, Hegel and Schelling elaborated it systematically. The so-called Lebensphilosophie of the earlier part of our century pursued the same theme though perhaps without bringing it into still clearer focus, since psychological interests clouded it.

The inquisitive child does not experience the psychological necessity of his question but its logical cogency.

The psychologist is merely confronted with his object. Natural necessity is something entirely different from the necessity of reason (Vernunftnotwendigkeit). The latter is itself the judging I.

> I deliberately translate this last sentence verbatim. One cannot strictly convert it and say the judging I is itself the necessity of reason (or the cogency of reason). For as a judging I, I am merely an instance of the all embracing cogency or necessity. To put it mythologically: I am not God but I find myself in God.

For psychology the contents of thought are merely represented, and the laws of thought are merely observed. But truth is immediate.

> This does precisely not mean that truth is a psychological fact. In 1805 Schelling wrote: "Reason is not a faculty, not a tool, it does not

let itself be used. Anyway there is no reason we could have but only a reason that has us. To seek in oneself any faculty of knowing God and to count or weigh such a faculty is the utmost degree of confusion and of innerdarkness of mind" (VII, 148f). And in seemingly mythological but really profoundly philosophical language, he continued: "Reason does not _have_ the idea of God, it _is_ that idea and nothing _else_" (ib. 149). -- It is an old story.Even the rationalist and objectivist St. Paul knew it when, as I quoted above (p. 3), he wrote: "Now I live, yet not I but Christ in me" (Gal.2:20). To be sure, as a rationalist he had to use mythological language. Augustine no longer had to do that. He could define immediacy by simply saying "nothing can be more present to itself" than I myself (_de Trinitate_ X, iii, 5). Kant wrote: "In the awareness of myself in sheer thought, I am the essence itself" and "the sentence _I exist as thinking_, is no mere logical function, but it determines the subject (which at the same time is object) with regard to its existence" (_Critique of Pure Reason_ 429). -- I am quoting all these things not in any endeavor to "prove" any proposition but in the hope that the reader will think for himself. Like 2+2=4 he must "add it up" for himself. Schelling wrote his Aphorism 31: "One cannot describe reason to anyone; it must describe itself in each and by each one" (VII, 146). And that is what Medicus means by immediacy. It is entirely beyond the reach of objectivism. It is within the reach even of a child.

Terminological distinction: immediate contents of thought/ represented contents of "consciousness".

I am putting the latter word in quotation marks because there is no such _thing_ as consciousness. There is only "_being_ conscious."

The contents of thought stand not in front of us like objects. We experience ourselves in these contents. As soon as the I detaches itself from the content of his thought, the latter becomes an object which lacks any inherent relation to truth. On the other hand, an I without content is an empty abstraction.

May 19 NECESSITY OF NATURE AND NECESSITY OF REASON

Consciousness (or: to _be_ conscious: Bewusst_sein_) is to be subject of its contents.

This requires explanation. But first I continue my translation.

The contents of THINKING (die Denkinhalte) can have only an immediate meaning; the thinking I is identical with its contents inasmuch as they are self-aware (selbstbewusst). Without contents the "I" is an empty abstraction. If a content is taken in isolation (for instance: mountain, gold) then of course it is not self-aware (selfconscious). It can be self-conscious only in its relations. Contents which are thinkable only in the immediacy in which they stand together in their specific interrelation of "thus and in no other way" (so und nicht anders) are they self-certain I. They are real thinking. Truth does not exist for itself; it is alive. In thinking there is self-aware (selbstbewusste) necessity as for instance in a mathematical proof. There is a trinity: I, truth, contents.

As soon as I represent (vorstelle) the contents of thought as contents of (an alleged) consciousness, I deprive them of their meaning which can be present only in immediacy. I can know only by immediate thinking. By means of merely represented contents of consciousness I know nothing.

Moreover the alive judgment (or proposition) cannot be taken apart. Subject and predicate are indivisibly one. What is taken apart in psychology is solely the sentence, the objectified connection of words.

HM Medicus had among his closer acquaintances the protestant pastor Oskar Pfister in Zürich, an early follower of Sigmund Freud (1856-1939). Medicus was very familiar with Freud's work.

Psychology cannot catch thinking in flagranti, that is, in the very act. Psychology must observe; it is a factual science. Therefore it is impossible that its object is the same as that of logic which does not deal with facts confronting us as objects (gegenüberstehende Tatsachen) but with the investigating I itself.

What requires an explanation is precisely the language Medicus uses on this page. He is speaking like a psychologist, in the abstract. One cannot really talk about thinking, nor about consciousness. One must on one's own perform the act of thinking to see its flagrant or blazing light. If one does not do that, all that is left of the flame are the words of the expressing sentence, the ashes as it were.

Thus the explanation must start from a specific or concrete thought which the reader can and is expected to think, on his own. In our case at hand, the reader has surely paused on the very first sentence: "To be conscious is to be subject of one's contents." If we parse that sentence we find that the grammatical subject is "consciousness" (whatever that word may mean), the simple copula is "is", and the predicate is "to be subject", specifically "subject of its contents." Thus it seems that there two distinguishable items, a subject (not in the grammatical but in the psychological sense) and its object, namely its contents. By using this kind of language I am making my reader objectify the matter at issue. I am inducing him to think psychologically. But that is precisely what Medicus does not want us to do.

Therefore let us start all over again. What has happened to us as we read the psychologizing language of Medicus? The specific or concrete content of Medicus' inquiry is our actual thinking. Now, as soon as we call it a process, that very word objectifies and psychologizes our problem and deprives it of its real question. The real question regards the "flagrant blaze" of thinking, if I may use this figure of speech. I am not speaking of a visible flame, but of that "inner light" which is lit as soon as we can honestly say: "Ah, I see what you mean!"

Medicus credits us with the ready ability to translate his psychologizing language into plain philosophical talk. And I am therefore taking the liberty of re-translating his page into terms that are not psychological and do not deviate myself nor the reader from the real problem: "What does thinking mean?"

Medicus speaks of the contents of consciousness in the plural. But we cannot think of anything unspecified nor of everything at the same time. We must focus on one specific content. (This does not deny the fact that one content calls for another and that we do look for the interrelation of all.) Medicus says in every real thought there is a trinity: "I, truth, content." In the first place I. As long as I am somnolent and drift in the stream of my daydreams (which may be very pleasant) I merely "go along". But to think means to pay attention to one content or topic, and to take the responsibility of setting aside whatever is not pertinent to that topic. To be a thinking I means to pause, look and listen. The observing psychologist speaks of "my consciousness" but he can ascertain its presence only by asking me: "Are you present?" If I am, I know it. Augustine reminded us that even if we dream we are aware of our presence (though not of the dream being "only a dream"). -- In the second place, I cannot be aware of the fact that it is I who am dreaming or thinking, unless I have a specific dream or thought, a specific "content". Yet, for the moment, that content is not one of two co-existent entities, my I and its content. True, in reflection I can distinguish them. But in reality I cannot be I without my content, nor can the specific content be a content of awareness without the aware I. --Thirdly, in mere daydreaming the two entities, I and my momentary content, merely happen to be co-existent. But to think means to ask for the necessity of that co-existence. (We ask: Why should I dream this? Or: Why are 2+2=4?) We ask for the truth, that is, for the specific truth that seems to be within our grasp, not for any truth in the abstract. There is no truth in the abstract. --Thus Medicus' trinity.

The I is "the subject of its content". In plain English: I know the topic of my thinking, at least in the form of a problem, though not yet in the form of an acceptable solution. But both, problem and solutions can be known only in the immediacy of I being I. The potentially knowable content becomes actually known, becomes "self-aware" in the student of it. (The Latin adjective studiosus means dedicated). The content is one, the students may be many. (2+2=4 is a content that comes to life again and again, in the minds of bright two or three year olds and, so we hope, surely for first graders.)

I cannot really understand a content except in its relations. The bright child who discovers that 2+2=4 is already fascinated by the magic of numbers. Furthermore contents are related to each other in "this and no other way," by what we may properly call the necessity of thought. Unlike the natural necessity, for instance of gravity or of electromagnetism, the necessity of thought is no mechanical objectivity. It can be apprehended only by the autonmous act of responsible thinking. It is a self-aware necessity. It exists only in thinking, not "by itself". (This is why a Platonizing theologian

> rightly says all the truths exist in the mind of God, "eternally.") Eternal means time-pervading.

When the potentially knowable becomes known in the form of a proposition (or of an entire scientific system) its meaning is identical with what the knower means. (This identity does not deny the distinction between the scientist and his system.)

> One might say the knower is the incarnate thinking.

Psychology cannot catch thinking in the act. But logic deals with the thinking I itself.

> This definition of logic is of course not the same as that of a still persisting school logic whose topics are abstract relationships. -- After the above long retranslation or transposition I go on with Medicus' remarks about all factual sciences.

Psychology is a factual science. For every factual science there must be a firm foundation in ascertainable and ascertained facts. Thus also in psychology facts must be taken as grounds for proofs.

Logic however can accept facts only as problems. It inquires into the significance of a fact for the knowledge of truth. The sciences are convinced that their ascertainment of facts serves truth. But logic must ask: What does the ascertaining of facts mean in historical or natural or some other science?

Every individual science (psychology among them) presupposes a logical insight into the ascertainment of its facts.

Psychologism is the assumption that psychology is the science which furnishes the basis for philosophy.

It is impossible that logic could presuppose psychological knowledge.

> Of course Medicus does not mean that a philosopher need not study psychology. That would be just as absurd as saying he need not know any physics, biology, geology, astronomy, history, art.

It is impossible because reason is not a fact. It is the presupposition of finding facts, of scientific objectivity.

Every objective necessity remains inwardly impenetrable for our knowledge. What is objective is contingent. And if we introduce rational constructions, for instance of a mathematical kind, they can only push back what is contingent and observable.

Necessity of thought must not and cannot be merely accepted (like the contingent). We can understand why it is necessary, why it is what it is. To be sure, it is a fact that errors of thought occur. But such offences do not impair the necessity of thought. In contrast, factual offences against ostensible law of nature refute the so-called law. --If a necessity of thought has been ascertained, it is entirely impossible to refute it. However that is not a coercion, for the thinking I discovers its own necessity by gaining insight into the ascertained necessity of thought.

> Many an academician will here loudly protest and call Medicus an unreconstructed idealist. However such protesters are unreconstructed believers in final formulations. They have not learned what Medicus learned from Kant and more especially from Fichte, Hegel and Schelling, that the ascertainment of a necessity of thought does indeed require a clear cut formulation but that such formulations inevitably use the language and the ideas available at the time. Therefore the formulations themselves call for a review when the times change. And in the review and by the review the unassailability of the necessity of thought reasserts itself.

The necessity of reason is no imposition on the I. It is identical with the living I. The I is not without "its law."

> If the reader needs an example let him remember the distinction between a priestly and a prophetic religion. The priestly religion clings to the clear cut formulation of an insight once attained. The result may strengthen a "chosen people" or an entire age. It may also choke a new life that needs reformulations. Hence the challenge of the prophets who speak in behalf of the Lord who can not be bound by any final formulations.
>
> Alive philosophy has always spoken in behalf of freedom and autonomy. Man is not to crouch and cringe. That is "God's law."

May 21

Natural necessity connects objects. Necessity of reason rests on itself.

> The form of natural necessity is "if then." The form of reason is "I am I." About objects we can

make mypotheses, produced by careful ratiocination. Reason is nothing hypothetical. Plato called it the non-hypothetical (anhypoteton) and Schelling said in 1805: "Reason cannot affirm anything that is real only in relation to or in comparison with something else (for if it did it would be the same as ratiocination). ...Reason can only posit what, in every regard and absolutely, is from itself and by itself or, in other words, what is the non-finite positing of itself" (VII, 167, aphorism 36). This, of course, is still academic language which sounds objectivistic, as if reason were an "it" and something far-fetched and puzzling. Augustine had long ago warned against such a surmise. He wrote of the mind (in his pithy Latin): "Non itaque velut absentem se quaerat cernere, sed praesentem se curet discernere" (de Trinitate X, ix, 12). Counter to his own warning, he still uses the feminine noun mens (from whose Sanscrit root the English noun mind derives, and from which our adjective mental derives directly). But Augustine also makes a perspicacious and pithy use of the contrast between the two verbs cernere, to sunder from among sundry hypothetical entities, and discernere, to keep an entity away from another with which it has nothing to do. The past participle of discernere is discretum, whence the English discrete. Webster says discreet means manifesting good judgment, but discrete means separate or individually distinct. In the latter sense I will use the word discrete as I try to translate Augustine's sentence as fittingly as I can. "Let the mind not seek to sort itself out as if it were one among sundry absent entities, but let it take care to find itself as individually discrete and present." If the reader finds this sentence stuffy and puzzling,let him remind himself that the topic is his self, that is, precisely what he means when, referring to his own self, he uses the only adequate and precise word "I", the personal pronoun in the first, that is, in his own person. No third person can tell him what the word "I" really means. He alone can tell. For nobody can substitute for him.

After this pedantic excursion into language and logic, let us return to the distinction between ratiocination, which can be either used or else ignored, and reason which can be neither used nor ignored. I quote again Schelling's aphorism 46 of 1805: "Reason is no faculty, no tool, and it cannot be used; anyhow there is no reason we could have but only a reason that has us" (VII, 148f). It "has us", not the way an obsession has us and enslaves us, but always as a liberator.

> Very young children take delight in the discovery of new colors, new sounds, even new tastes, and in all new things. Discovering them they discover the richness of their own lives. When they enter their questioning age, they delight in finding tenable answers (which, to be sure, may prove untenable later on). What they discover in any meaningful "truth" is precisely the "necessity of reason", that is, the power and autonomy of their mind, the fact that they can and must think for themselves. The "necessity of reason" is no objective fate like the necessity of nature. It is their own freedom, the liberty of their intellect.

Without perceptual contents the I would remain empty, but _in_ the contents the I seeks itself. The greater the wealth of (initially chaotic) representations, the richer the I. For instance, in the very young child there is a chaos of perceptions and subjective mental conditions. Then the I detaches these contents from itself. The subjective sensation "red" is replaced by the "red thing." The child experiences himself more distinctly, the more he ascertains objective necessities.

> This is especially obvious in the discovery of the objective limits of his bodily potentialities. Though the limits may be frustrating, there is always the prospect of "what I'll do when I'm bigger."

The awareness of objective necessity may not be accompanied by the explicit insight into its necessity. It may be only an awareness of a mute, dull, muffled necessity (dumpfe Notwendigkeit).

> _Dumpf_ was a favorite word of Medicus. It has no precise English equivalent. "Ein dumpfer Ton" is a muffled sound like distant thunder. The not very frequent adjective "fusty" would come close, if we could get rid of the first meaning found in Webster, "moldy, musty, rank", and restrict it to the second, "without freshness of life."

Yet even this fusty awareness is in the I, not in the object.

FORMAL LOGIC and the LOGIC OF CONCRETE THINKING

Down to Kant the opinion was nearly undisputed that logic must deal with the mere form of thinking, with ratiocination abstracting from its contents. This formal logic observed only the "quantity" (universal, particular, individual) and the so-called "quality" (affirmative, negative) of a judgment or proposition. The opinion was dominant that the formal laws of thinking are selfevident. Objective thinking was considered secondary. Even Kant still declared that logic is so perfect a science because in logic ratiocination is concerned only with itself. Moreover all objects could introduce only perplexities.

In contrast, the logic of concrete thinking (or logic of content) shows that a ratiocination that deals only with itself is a meaningless abstraction. Any content must evolve from a subjective condition in the mind to an objectivity independent of the mind. Only confronted by that Not-I can the I get a hold of itself. Every new problem of thought signifies anew, that the I must come forth from its entanglement in what is strange, by means of placing the strange in its proper location in the objective domain.

In short: I cannot think without thinking something. Formal logic sees in the place of this something nothing but reason itself. But the necessity of reason is alive only in the contents of thought. (Thus, for instance, the chess player is outside the chess figures, but he lives in them, and in both, the black as well as the white ones.)

> There seems to be a gap in my notes. They omit the naive question: What kind of a thing is the I? The answer of course is: No thing. And indeed, for the objectivist the I is nothing. That, for objectivistic thinking is quite true. Kant's followers told why.

Fichte says: "The I is a doing, not a doer." In formal logic it is a doer.

> Formal logic describes the behavior pattern of a doer. The pattern can then be copied and built into a computer, which is a pure doer and no I at all, no sheer doing. -- Medicus illustrates:

(The real chess player is a doing in his game.) As soon as we conceive of consciousness as an object, the living I recedes from that object, by means of the very act by which the object is conceived.

The contents of thinking are alive, for the I or reason is in them. Only thereby are they contents of thinking. Evidence can be found only in self-aware contents of thinking.

The validity of the ostensibly "self-evident laws of thinking" manifests itself only in the doing or active organizing of contents of thinking. The whole meaning of laws of thinking is found only in concrete contents of thinking, only where these contents seek the truth of their interrelationship. If we speak of principles of thinking independent of any content, we indulge in abstraction and objectification. The "principles" are manifest only in immediate thinking.

Wherever they are alive, these "principles" cannot at all be re-presented, for they prove themselves only in the immediacy of actual thinking. One cannot align one's thinking with a contentless "principle" of causality, or the "principle of contradiction." For instance, the proposition "he died because the little owl cried last night" cannot be corrected "in line with" an abstract principle of causality.

> What the owl's cry can actually cause is apprehension, uneasyness, fear. These may undermine the mental resistance to death. But the physical cause of death is a medical not a psychological problem. To be sure the two are related, but not by the cry of the owl.

May 26

What is necessary for any explanation is the connection of the case at hand with the reality of reason. In other words, one cannot think without thinking something. The formal "laws of thinking" are meaningless if they do not refer to something specific. Reason is the necessity found in the contents of thinking. Reason is the self-certainty of truth. That does not mean at all that some kind of "law" is forced upon the specific thing. Our knowledge of things reaches precisely as far as the reach of self-certain necessity in our consciousness, for that necessity is of the essence of things. That rules out the point of view of skepsis that would be expressed in saying "we know only so much." On the contrary, we know that much of the essence of things. (The word "we" here means the self-certain truth.)

Of course there are specific limits of knowledge, for instance the limitation of our senses. But to point them out is not the same as a general skepsis, in whose refutation we must say the following.

The very essence of things (das Wesen der Dinge) attains self-certainty. To know means to ascertain truth. Therefore in knowing things everything contingent and arbitrary must drop by the wayside. The essence of things is nothing that transscends our logical experience (das logische Erleben). Things are the content of thinking. These contents demand our acknowledgment of their interrelationships which are "thus and not otherwise," in line with the necessity of truth. This necessity is what things are.

> In academic jargon, assertions like these have been called absolute idealism. The latter word derives from idea which in turn derives from the Greek verb idein, to see. "Idea" means a sight. And any sight or insight is an alive event, not a dead object. The "event" is not an evanescent psychological moment, although it does occur in time. It is what Medicus would call "supertemporal" (überzeitlich) which means that the validity of the idea does not depend on the temporal circumstances but, on the contrary, is time pervasive. This is why Plato called his realm of ideas the "real world", in contrast to the sense world which passes away. And this is also why scientists rightly feel that the laws they discover are of the essence of things, though always open to checking and rewording. --Kant pointed out that his "transcendental idealism" is also "empirical realism" and that, in contrast, the realism of objectivistic metaphysics is the same thing as the empirical idealism, e.g. of Berkeley.

By means of abstraction one can turn things into "things in themselves" (Dinge an sich) and turn real thinking into "laws of thinking by itself." But those are two abstractions, not two realities. In reality, thinking and being are not separated.

> And that, of course, is what Parmenides first discovered when the insight came upon him that isness is the cogency of "cannot not be" and therefore the same as the cogency of thought.

When abstraction separates thinking and being, the following misunderstandings arise.

1) The copy theory declares that it is impossible to compare a representation with the thing in itself ostensibly represented. Therefore truth cannot be ascertained but is simply beyond our reach. This granted, what follows is 2) the Theory of establishing order among representations by means of thinking. That would ascertain the agreement among the conformity of representations in line with "laws of thinking." However such conformity of representations would not bring us closer to reality. The consequence is solipsism, which Fichte and Schopenhauer call "Theoretical egoism." The word comes from

solus ipse, nothing but oneself. Solipsism takes its clue from Descartes' cogito ergo sum, I am aware therefore I am. Solipsism teaches that I have only my representations. However, critical reflection will remind us that, for actual immediate thinking, the "I" as individual is also nothing but content of thought. The "I think" is already a thinking of me. The immediate thought has no relation to my individuality, my me, for it makes no difference whether its content be some other object or the "I" as individual. The immediate concern of thinking is only the fact that the contents of thought demand to be thought together "in this and no other way." I am an individual only as an object or content of thought.

The logical subject itself is impersonal. The individual is not the living I, the alive logical subject; it is its content. The logical subject is not an individual.

> This is why thinking immediately establishes mutual understanding. When a class recites in unison, it is a symbolic expression of the superindividual unity established by the truth of what is recited. (Of course some of the pupils in the class may absent-mindedly merely make the sounds of the recital. And, in case of bad teaching, the entire class may go home with the impression that all they are to learn is making the sounds. The same happens, sad to say, with regard to church rituals which are meant as symbols of "the Spirit" and yet may turn out, in the members' minds, nothing but making sounds.) --Perhaps the best illustration of superindividual unity is an orchestra or a really good theatrical performance. Each musician or each actor makes his or her own sounds, yet they can all experience the unity of the musical piece or the play. And the purpose of the performance is that the unity embrace the audience beyond the footlights.

What is immediately certain are not the contents of my individual mind, my representations, but the unity of content of thought. An isolated content "of thought" is meaningless if separated from the act of thinking. What makes the contents immediately certain is not their presence in a consciousness but the necessity of their relationship. This necessity assigns to the contents their definite place in time and space. It likewise assigns the proper place to the individual.

> As an individual I find myself at home, most of the time, in the German of Medicus, in the present case in his classroom of 1919. Yet I am now some sixty

> years older and am sitting at my typewriter, with a view of the St. Joseph River at the foot of the bluff of St. Mary's College. My task is not to transpose my notes into English but to find an English expression for the superindividual truths Medicus voiced in 1919 in the southwest corner classroom on the second floor of the Polytechnikum in Zürich, with a view of the lake and the Alps.

As contents of real thinking the thought contents belong to the logical, not to the individual I.

> And without exception all we individuals live in the logical I, although in many regards each one of us may not yet have matured and as yet be a merely potential member of the community of the logical I. --Unless we happen to be mongoloid morons, we ought to take ourselves in hand and do our duty to study.

May 28

Solipsism must indeed call all talk about entities beyond representation mere unfounded metaphysics. However, as stated before what is immediately certain are not "my" representations but their living contents. Solipsism is a relinquishment of truth, that is, of the original meaning of the contents of thinking. What we call our "object" is the unity of subjective feelings, sensations, perceptions, that is, mental conditions which, if taken separately, are heterogeneous; the necessity of a thought however comprehends them in a synthetic unity.

> A literal minded Kantian, though not Kant himself, would say that these as yet unapprehended mental conditions are the raw material which is fed into the shaping mechanism of the mind which first places the material into time and space and then shapes it by means of the mind's innate forms, the categories, thus shaping the object as a substance whose changes have measurable causes, etc. But such a Kantian is no longer dealing with the life of what is really known. He talks like an objectifying psychologist for whom every mental condition is of psychological interest, regardless of truth or error. The last sentence of Medicus is in danger of being misread as if he were psychologizing like the Kantians.

As soon as we ask ourselves "What does this mean?" the merely subjective condition of feeling or sensation becomes an object. thus, for instance, a sensation of light.

> I wake up in the middle of the night with such a sensation and I immediately say to myself it must have been the headlights of a car which shone into my bedroom.

In a very young baby the logical consciousness is still dormant. Thus the baby is not yet aware of objects, only of subjective mental conditions. However this is not a matter of two successive logical experiences, as if the baby were first aware of being in a merely subjective condition and then became aware of an objective interpretation. The baby is in his condition but is not aware of its subjectivity. As soon as I am aware of the condition as _mine_, it already stands in relation to reality.

> This is why we are so delighted with the baby's first smile which indicates that the baby is aware of his "being here" and likes it or, more presicely, likes the company.

Logical consciousness is aware of anything only because it is aware of its meaning. _The relation to reality is logically primary_. The object is secondary, because it becomes object only in distinction from the individualized I.

> In brackets, my notes say: Now I can see the possibility of the existence of a psychology that deals with a consciousness without meanings. When Medicus uses the example of a sleep disturbing sensation of light, to illustrate an as yet meaningless sensation, he lifts logic into an _entirely_ peculiar sphere proper to it alone and otherwise inaccessible. But _outside_ of logic there would be room for psychology.

The subject of logical knowledge is _not_ the individual. The individual is an object. _Truth has us; we do not have it_.

> Medicus must have thought of Schelling's Aphorism 46: "There is no reason we could have but only a reason that has us" (VII, 149).

To be sure, we can betray truth, but lies are the topic of ethics not of logic. The contents of thought are individual, but truth lies in the _meaning_ of the contents, and that meaning is superindividual. Truth lies not in nerve impressions but in the necessity that, for logical consciousness, the contents are contents of thinking, and thinking is the apprehension (Erfassen) of objects.

Thinking is not a function of the individual; it means to be grasped by a superior necessity that dwells in the things themselves.

> This superiority is by no means a coercive power but a liberating invitation. Hence our delight in discovering a truth.

In thinking, man experiences the essence (Wesen) of things. Their meaning is immediately certain.

> Of course Medicus does not mean an immediacy that can dispense with the labor of research. Even if a scientist has a flash of inspiration he will not stop but conscientiously think of all possible objections and of possible crucial experiment.

Every meaning is a specific shape (Gestalt) of the truth that grasps itself. Meaning has the form of I (ist ichhaft) and at the same time the essence of the object. It is unity of the subjective and the objective. Meaning is the reasonability (das Venünftige) in things.

Truth knows no limits. There is nothing that could exist independent of truth. With regard to anything that concerns us in any way we can legitimately ask for its meaning.

> Hence the unconditional freedom of thought is a basic human right.

Reality cannot withhold itself from truth. By necessity "what is real is reasonable" (was wirklich ist, das ist vernünftig) said Hegel.

> Significantly in the preface to his Philosophy of Right, June 25, 1820. And, without asking "What does this mean?", without studying Hegel, and above all without heeding Kant's distinction between reason and ratiocination, Hegel's self-styled critics jumped to the conclusion that Hegel meant to deny the fact that not everything is neatly rational, not every human act legal nor morally right. These academics forget that the expression Wrath of God is not nonsense and need not mean the anger of a bossy god.

THE NATURE OF ERROR, THE GROWTH OF CONCEPTS, AND FORMAL LOGIC

How then is error (Falsches) possible? Error challenges us to ascertain the lack of truth in it. Spinoza said "there is nothing positive in the ideas, on account of which they could be false."

> Ethics, II, Prop. xxxiii: Nihil in ideis positivum est, propter quod falsae dicuntur.

The falsehood does not lie in the elements of thought as such (e.g. blue, wet, etc.) nor in their theoretical interrelation, but "l'errore è nel permanere dove si passa solo" (Benedetto Croce, in the first edition of his Logica.)

> Error lies in stopping where one should go farther. --This marks modernity from medievalism to which Galilei still adhered when he said error means not to quiet oneself in the true - "il non si quietar nel vero."

Whatever makes a false kind of thinking a thought is true; thought is never entirely false. But the one who errs has not pushed the movement of thinking far enough.

The one who really knows is safe only from those errors he himself has overcome; the danger through which he passed no longer threatens him. In contrast, the positively correct insight wavers if it is known only as a result without its grounds. He who does not know the grounds of his knowledge can be disturbed by the one who is in error, because in the latter's grounds there is always some reason. As soon as the knowing one grasps the intention and meaning of the one in error, he can refute him.

Error grows in the domain of truth in the making. Without truth there is no error.

June 2

Error grows in the domain of truth in the making. These words do not mean that truth grows from error. To err means to stop at some single reasoning (Begründung). Now selfcertain truth does live only in and through it reasons (Gründe). Therefore concrete logic cannot separate knowledge, that is, the logical meaning of a judgment or proposition from its grounds, as formal and abstract logic does. The title of being true (das Wahrheitsrecht) pertaining to a judgment or proposition does not lie in its form. The life of truth must slip from the grasp of formal logic.

Knowing this, Kant says that a judgment or proposition could connect concepts in a way which "the object (Gegenstand) does not bring along" (mit sich bringt) and, thus, although being formally correct, would be groundless.

See Critique of Pure Reason, 1781

Formal logic can rise up only against inner contradictions. A groundless judgment (lacking any ground in concrete thought) has no real meaning although it is not false. But even in a meaningful judgment formal logic can discover only its lack of inner contradiction. If it lacks grounds, a connection of concepts is not an accomplishment of ratiocination (des Verstandes) but of fantasy. In such a case an act of sheer will juxtaposes what ratiocination could readily recognize as far fetched and lacking any real connection. For instance, the proposition "quadrilaterals are not married" only looks like a judgment but is meaningless.

> Even a bright child would call this a game of words and might ask: What is the use of wasting breath on it?

Benedetto Croce demands a sharp distinction between grammar and logic. If one takes meaningless though grammatically correct connections of words for judgments, one can no longer understand what it really means to connect concepts. Concepts are no chess figures which remain whatever they are. A real judgment lives and is nourished by its grounds. The concept grows in the judgment and becomes richer. For instance, before we study geometry we have a concept of a triangle. That concept is not false and has not been wiped out by geometry, but after the study it is manifestly more mature; it has grown.

Such growth of concepts occurs in all domains of thinking. For instance, new grounds will confirm our concept of an historical personality. And like a geometric concept it may attain necessity and become a concept of historical discipline.

Predication is no mere collocation of subject and predicate. The two become one. And after the predication the two confront each other as being both more than before the predication. After it, we can no longer conceive as little in both of them as we did before.

> If the reader requires an example let him reread this last paragraph and ask himself whether or not the word predication now means more.

Formal logic puts great stress on the [affirmative or negative] "quality" of a judgment. However significance or meaning is always positive (and without meaning a judgment is worthless). Movements of thought always pass over mere negations. To be sure, even in an affirmative judgment there is a negative moment or significance, because subject and predicate do not simply fuse in the predication. They remain distinct, and their unity is one of tension. It is a challenge to us. No judgment is a final conclusion.

June 4

All meaning is necessarily positive. Negation however points beyond itself. Therefore knowledge is without termination, for in everything positive there is also some negation. (Purely negative human beings are merely set aside. We cannot say we have prevailed over them.)

ON THE CUSTOMARY PRESENTATION OF SOCALLED LAWS OF THOUGHT

1) Law of identity: "If A is, then there is A." This makes sense for instance when we distinguish between several distinct meanings of one and the same word and point out which one of these meanings we have in mind when we use the word. The real sense of the law says: Thinking means reason's becoming aware of itself. Fichte says A=A is meaningful not as a mere formula but as a form of stating that "I am I", that is, of the selfcertainty of reason. In other words: "If A means I, then I know what reason means."

> Provided of course that I have mastered the basic discipline of philosophical reflection and thus have come to know that I as I am not an object.

Otherwise the formula remains empty. The necessity of thought is certain of itself. And such identity of meaning is in every kind of knowledge. For instance the addition of a series of numbers. Of course the meaning of the resulting number must be known, otherwise the solution is impossible. Thus a child who does not yet know the words with which we name the numbers cannot follow the argument of our adding the numbers.

> Another example would be the case of a pupil who just enters into algebra. He clings to specific numbers but is willing to compromise and say, for instance, a for eleven, b for twelve, etc. But he dares not let go of such specific numerical value of a, b, c, etc. He has not yet mastered the skill of abstraction which rests on this Law

> of Identity: "If a is a, then it means a and nothing else", that is, in this game of algebra.

The really adding child comes to see the identity of the sum of the series with the resulting number.

Another example: "Gold is an element." In order to understand this sentence we must know what the word element means. Then only can we see the identity of "gold" and "one of the elements." Every meaning is a shape (Gestalt) of reason which experiences its own identity in that meaning. In chemistry "Na + Cl = NaCl" means that, under certain conditions, Na and Cl can be identical with NaCl.

To recognize change means to recognize the identical, the meaning.

Again, to "understand the action of some human" means to recognize his or her character (the identity) in the action.

There is no I hovering above the contents of thinking, moving them around like a chessplayer who moves his figures. Concepts are no fixed figures and cannot be held fast as the expression "to hold on to one's concepts" would seem to mean. The contents of thought organize themselves, and that is what their "identity" should mean. Real thinking precludes any surreptitious change of meaning, for the connection of contents of thought is necessary. Thus no different meanings can slip in. Yet the concepts cannot be "held fast" without change. That would mean a relinquishment of thinking. In thinking concepts become richer, they are not chess figures.

In sum: a) A=A is not a principle, not self-evident, but evident only as I=I. b) The "law" is not a prescription for thinking, no dead "instruction". c) Furthermore concepts have no rigidly fixed identity.

2) Law of contradiction: "A is not non-A" is sometimes called a prohibition (Verbot). Sheer identity would be dead. But since real identity is alive, it contains distinction. The "I am I" drives beyond itself.

> Fichte's sentence "as I, I am for myself alone" ends on the word alone which immediately points at some not-I.

To be sure, "I am I" is alive identity, but it does not exclude distinction though it does not explicitly mention it. The I knows itself only insofar as it knows at the same time a not-I. Therefore "not-I is not I."

Insofar as anything is knowledge it has the form of I, be it whatever it is, for instance gold, or the Üetliberg (the mountain west of Zürich visible from the room in which Medicus lectured; he probably pointed at it). The meaning of the known entity is at the same time selfawareness of the I as well as distinction between the I and the known thing.

Knowledge is movement, alive experience of meaning, not rigid representation.

> The reader should remind himself that the German word Vorstellung literally means to stand something up in front of oneself, like a stick or marker. And indeed, taken as dead psychological facts, representations are only rigid markers.

Our every grasping of a meaning creates new contents, but not new objects, for our representations are all in some way abstractions; the objects remain objects. There are people who "know a lot" or even "know it all". To really know much means to have more contents, more concepts.

Scientific research in any discipline has as its essential purpose not the search for new objects but for new relationships among the old objects. For example the search not for new details of the time of 1792 but for a new and deeper meaning of the Revolution.

> The date here jumps from June 4 to June 16, presumably on account of the Pentecost vacation.

June 16

Contents of thought retain their identity in their life, however as they live they transform themselves.

If its contents are set aside, the I is an abstraction to which neither an order nor a prohibition can be addressed, and which knows no "law" of thought. The lawfulness which lives in the contents of thought is no rigid being-thus, once and for all. The identity of the content always points beyond itself.

> Consequently the content as it is before its self-transformation can be distinguished from what it is afterwards.

Such distinction, at first glance, appears as a self-estrangement. Similarly, in the current of our life, we become estranged from ourselves. Nietzsche says "nur wer sich wandelt, bleibt mir selbst verwandt;" only he who changes remains akin to me. And this estrangement is the more pronounced the more intensely we live. Similarly, concepts become estranged. If a man were to live a thousand years and always keep himself at the height of the time, he would have to learn anew most of what he knows. Nevertheless he would remain identical with himself, precisely because of his steady self-estrangement. To be sure it would not be the flat identity of A=A. As we continuously learn anew during our life, our identity is true to our selves; it is historical. Similarly the self-identity of a concept is historical. This similarity is no mere comparison, although it is a crude manifestation of the problem that regards the "growth" of a concept.

Every act of thinking contains a relation to reality. The forms of thought are nothing by themselves. They become meaningless the moment their relation to reality is set aside. Every abstraction is meaningful as long as it is still related to reality. However reality, even in its smallest parts, cannot be exhausted by no matter what amount of moves of thinking. Reality remains fact even when we attain insight into its deeper depth. What remains is a "being-thus" which ratiocination must simply accept, a not-I confronting the I. In experiencing meaning the I knows something of itself but only by also simultaneously knowing of a not-I. It knows something of the latter yet must distinguish it from its own self as something that remains strange.

The movement of knowing is like a one-dimensional line which penetrates a three-dimensional space. Without reality no penetrating thought is possible. An I is possible only through a not-I. The not-I confronts the I as an infinite task.

In and by itself the I is self-certain necessity (or cogency).

> The English word necessity seems to retain a trace of "need" and a more perceptible trace of "fate", even "coercion". Of the latter there is a trace in "cogency," unless we qualify specifically the "cogency of thought" which is no coercion but liberation of mind. The German Denknotwendigkeit seems quite free of such coercive traits. Hence my warning to the reader.

There is a kind of dialectic contradiction which needs to be expounded as follows. Truth is absolutely self-certain, it is unconditionally. Therefore the not-I is nothing final; it is something that must be overcome. The not-I has not the same title or right as the unconditional truth. Therefore it is not a "thing in itself." It is not the Devil alongside and on the same line with God. Only the truth has ultimate validity. In dealing with what it wants to penetrate, the movement of thought sets itself a barrier which must be stepped over. The self-certainty of truth is no pure affirmation, rather it is a life, that is, a continued stepping over ever new negatives. Problems which are still uncertain are not yet ripe, but the present moment demands that we work on whatever is comprehensible in the problem. That is why in every present problem we experience a conscious self-estrangement, and in the solution of the problem a renewed self-certainty.

June 18

Croce stresses the "unità" of the one principio dell'identità e distinzione."

> There is but one principle, not the ostensible two of identity and of distinction (or contradiction).
>
> In the third edition (of 1917) of the Logica page 57 has the marginal subtitle: L'unità-distinzione como circolo. Croce argues, "in order that the concept be unity in distinction and be comparable to an organism it is necessary that none of the terms" be first or last. As in a circle one can start from any one point and, having gone around, arrive back at it. "In the organism, in fact, no member has priority over the others, but each in turn is both first and last." They are all distinct, yet in the organic unity.

The meaning of the "law of contradiction" is that the negative gets negated. Our knowledge of reality is never finished. However, specific definite problems can really be solved. For example "the blindworm is not a snake" requires the completion "but it is a lizard;" yet this completion is not an end, for it brings forth further questions.

Why does this specific kind of lizard lack legs?

The known and the problematic complement each other to the totality of the knowable. Formal logic calls it contradictory disjunction (a complete subdivision into contrasts).

The as yet unknown is a task. From its relation to the known formal logic derived its so-called

3) law of the excluded third, without knowing that this law is merely derivative. Its Latin form is: omne A aut B aut non B; every A is either B or not B. Since everything necessarily belongs to the domain of truth, no non-B can entirely withdraw from being knowable. Therefore statements can be made about it. In truth, the unknown is a task. Instead of live truth formal logic grasps only the meaningless though correct statement that in every pair of contradictory statements one must be "true". (The second "law" said they cannot both be true.) Real

thinking has no concern with the monster non-B. "Not-snake" is as yet nothing true but at best a task to be investigated. Non-B abstracts from content and is nothing but form. The third "law" is a mere abstraction from the second.

4) The law of sufficient ground

August Stadler was the predecessor of Medicus at the Institute.

Stadler's Logic says: "A judgment is necessarily correct only through its relation to other judgments, in line with the laws of thinking." This theorem conceives of judgments quite differently from the three first "laws." Stadler says the word "sufficient" is superfluous; Croce however has the word sufficiente printed in bold letters, because for real knowledge it is not enough to present just any reason. Self-certainty rests on real reasons, not on just any reason.

Probability

Most hypotheses of natural science have reasons which are correct but which are not entirely sufficient. The things are not (yet) thought in their truth. Another example: A juridical proof based on circumstantial evidence is not "sufficient", nevertheless its grounds are not "non-grounds" as formal logic would say.

A judgment of genuine knowledge is more than probable. However, this heading does not cover mathematical probability which, in its own field, has its sufficient grounds. Yet as soon as one steps forth from this merely mathematical probability into reality from which that probability abstracted, one is back in the field of the problematic, e.g. of roulette.

Every judgment is simultaneously affirmative and negative, and both moments demand their grounds; therefore one ground is not yet sufficient. The law of sufficient ground signifies something much more comprehensive than formal logic would admit when it first enumerates three laws and then a fourth about contexts. Without its grounds a judgment is meaningless. Meaning is found only in thinking the grounds. The fourth "law" is only a condensation of 1) and 2). It really says that the life of truth has its grounds in itself.

Insofar as no judgment or proposition can linguistically fix knowledge as absolutely (schlechthin) true, no judgment is sufficiently grounded; none contains in itself the truth. The principle of sufficient reason places every judgment into the endless process of the life of truth.

June 23 IMPERSONAL PROPOSITIONS AS ELEMENTARY JUDGMENTS

It is true that a proposition like "electricity has an atomic structure" is grammatically simple. Concepts do comprise movements of thinking which may be very complex, yet in a judgment they are used as units. This use makes it possible to say much in few words. -- The distinction between confused and clear minds rests essentially on their knowledge of the conceptual prehistory of the elements of a judgment.

What are the truly elementary movements of thinking? -- There are "impersonal" statements or subjectless sentences like "it lightens." Such sentences do not yet work up reality conceptually. They make an immediate statement, as yet without reflection. Logically "it" is not a subject. In Italian, for instance, there is no such personal (or rather impersonal) pronoun but the verb occurs in the third person singular: "lampeggia." However this kind of expression is no mere representation (Vorstellung; better: presentation). It does have the form of a judgment, and a judgment requires both, subject and predicate, it has a plural content. A presentation has only one content. Linguistically we find a verbal stem with a personal ending, and that ending [e.g. in Latin "fulgurat" or "fulminat"] has the function of a logical predicate. In this case the subject, expressed by the verbal stem, has no individuality and therefore needs no separate word. "It lightens" does not mean "this particular stroke of lighting" is what lightens over there. It means merely the fulguration which has no individuality. One does not usually say "one stroke of lightning struck here, another over there", but simply (the) lightning struck. The logical subject of that judgment is the impersonal power of lightning. Such impersonal judgments are not restricted to statement about the weather. We also say "its smokes" (for "there is smoke") or "it is haunting". However these judgments do not presuppose concepts like lightning, hail, ghosts. A child needs to be told only the name of lightning, in order to be able to understand the proposition "it lightens", no concept ("lightning") is needed.

> HM "It lightens" may be translated figuratively with "flash of insight."

Names are not logical but aesthetical creations. Therefore one cannot call language "true" or "false". The glow of creative originality can vanish in worn out words which have been used to designate ever new contents and which so lose their expressiveness. Of course they also gain more varied meanings.

Not the abstraction "lightning" is the logical subject of "it lightens" but rather the concreteness of the natural power. "It lightens" tells us no more about the essence of lightning than, for instance, what the child knows of "Saint Nicolas" whom the child knows only as a presence, not as a concept.

> Medicus refers to the Swiss custom that lets someone impersonate the good saint on the evening of December 6. I have been told that our maid did a creditable impersonation when I was very little. Of course the custume was not the American department store red, but wood sole farm shoes, brown old mantel, fur cap, as realistic a beard as possible. Nor did our "Samichlaus" come from the North Pole. We children never asked where he lived. He simply came. Not with reindeers (I still do not know how they ever got into the act) but with a sensible modest donkey. Farm children would set out a small bundle of hay for it. Its disappearance was proof that the donkey had eaten it. Samichlaus was never so stupid as trying to come down a chimney flue. He stomped in by the door. When my brother and I had reached the age in inquisitiveness, while our sister was still three or four, her godfather did the impersonation. Ten minutes later he rang our door bell out of costume and was very sorry he had missed the "Samichlaus" whom, so he said, he had not seen in a long time. Swiss fashion, he shook hands all around. He had the peculiar habit of giving the shaken hand a little twist. My brother and I merely glanced at each other, and our glance was the logical expression of our conceptual discovery: There really is no Samichlaus. We had the decency of not robbing our sister of her illusion.

The child knows Samichlaus but not as a concept. The abstract term "lightning" expresses an essence. But impersonal propositions do not inquire into essences. They merely acknowledge an immediate reality. Thinking is always concerned with what is real.

In this respect, Croce's view is unsatisfactory. He is of the opinion that impersonal propositions evoke only an intuition (Anschauung).

> Perhaps I should translate "only an image," (to say illusion would be wrong).

No, that is what the poet evokes. But the impersonal proposition is a statement about reality. When in Lessing's "Nathan der Weise", in the seventh scene of the third act, the wise Nathan begins to tell the Sultan Saladin a tale, "Vor grauen Jahren lebt' ein Mann im Osten", it is no statement about reality.

> One might say Nathan paints a picture gray in gray --"gray years ago there lived a man in the east" --not in realistic colors. -- The tale is about the magic ring that came down from father to son till one father had the weakness of promising the ring to each of his three sons. He had two imitations made so perfect that he himself could not distinguish them from the original. After his death each brother claimed to have the original. The judge decided that each should keep his ring in good faith and that, in a thousand years, the descendants should appear in court with the evidence that the original made the faithful bearer beloved by man and God. -- The parable of the ring signifies the three religions of Judaism, Christianity and Islam.

Many logic textbooks designate impersonal propositions as "existential". However these propositions are not statements about existence in general. They merely state a purely present existence, and more specifically they state an event, not a "being" as Herbart mistakenly asserts when he claims that "it lightens" means "there is (such a thing) as lightning". "It lightens means that the event of lighten-ing is occurring. Logically the two propositions "it strikes" and "the clock strikes" mean the same. "The clock" is here not an abstract concept but merely a name; if language permitted, one could say "it clockstrikes." Of course if anyone should have asked the causal question: What strikes? then the conceptual answer (pedantically lengthened) would be: "It is the clock that strikes."

Impersonal propositions have validity which is restricted temporally and spatially. Yet the sentence itself does not express this limitation. It looks as if it were generally valid, absolutely true. Only if we turn away from the now and here and try to read the proposition as if it had general validity, can we see it has not. Because then we reflect on the proposition or judgment. And it is this reflection which makes clear to us the extent of validity. The impersonal proposition express the limitation of its validity.

> One might insert a corollary. The religions demand what they call "having faith." They demand that the faithful live in his present experience of the "saving" value of the myth, that is, the poetic reality of the imagery of the myth. The religions do not like to call it myth, for they are afraid that the inquisitive mind might raise the conceptual question regarding the range of validity. The religions realize implicitly that the saving value covers only the faithful. The "infidels" look at the myth from the outside and, if they have been intellectually mistutored by our careless language, then they will say that "this imagery is only a myth", thus abusing the venerable word myth.--When Vatican II put most of its emphasis on the liturgy, I was first perplexed. But liturgy is religion in practice, not in "detached" theologizing. The myth is real in the immediacy of life, in its present event.

Only when we reflect that every presence promptly plunges into the past, --

> Exodus 33-23 says "you shall see my back, my face shall not be seen"

--only then can we see the limitation of the elementary judgment, in which time and space are limits that are not explicitly expressed in the proposition itself. The elementary judgment formulates a truth which promptly becomes untrue. Yet this negativeness is what must be overcome. And it can be overcome by placing the elementary judgment into a context of judgments which can and does retain what is true in that first immediacy.

June 25 THE CONTEXT OF JUDGMENTS AND THE KINDS AND DEGREES OF REALITY

The task of seeking a verifying context of judgments consists in recognizing the existence of the momentary in a lasting existence. In order to do that, we must know that there are kinds and degrees of reality, of existence.

Logic seeks the insight into the organism of the various sciences or disciplines, that is, into the various kinds of existential domains. For instance, physics and chemistry deal with the same kind of reality, history with quite another. One and the same object can be related to different spheres. For instance, to say "there is no four dimensional space" does not mean there is none in mathematics. In mathematics it exists [but not in our ordinary experience of three dimensional space contrasted by time]. To say "God alone is" means to assert a highest concept of reality as a measure in comparison with which everything else appears as ma on, not-being. Negative judgments do not deny lower ways of existence, because nothing at all could be predicated of absolute not-being.

Affirmative judgments place the logical subject into a higher sphere of existence. For instance, the proposition "the non-Euclidean space exists" means it exists not only in mathematics.

One should take care not to be deceived by the grammatical form of propositions. What they mean is never any isolated subject, but always the specific context of reality in which the subject stands. An existential proposition says in which sphere the thing and the thought of it are one. The methodical problem has attained actuality through Kant.

Existence is not a predicate like all others. To say "this piece of chalk exists" is ultimately a proposition about reality as such (Wirklichkeit überhaupt).

> To translate überhaupt as in general is too vague and too weak.

The proposition about the piece of chalk says that its existence occurs in reality as such. And the proposition about non-Euclidean space says the same. The proof of the latter existence requires a profusion of investigations concerning physical and astronomical contexts.

Our senses offer no guarantee that we are not victims of illusion. Already Heraclitus pointed that out. Eventually Descartes made it clear that certainty is found only in self-certainty.

> Now, in 1981, I wonder why Medicus, in 1919, did not remind us that, elevenhundred years before Descartes, Augustine put it even more clearly.

The senses are by no means superfluous, but what they furnish is always some not-I, that is, some task for our inquiry.

Only a really comprehended fact (begriffene Tatsache) can furnish the ground of proof for the specific kind of existence. This kind of fact is found only by placing the sense report into the proper contexts of reality, for instance in case of the question: "Have I only dreamed that?"

The proof of the existence of something perceived lies in the selfcertain necessity of a context which is "thus and no other way." Then concept and reality are one and the same.

At this point Medicus did not go into the logic of "identity." —The flat and really insipid identity of A=A has but a minimal logical weight. "if A is A, then A is A" is so poor a truth that almost anybody will say: "Why mention it?" But meaningful identity always contains distinction also. (Even A=A does not have the conventional sign, the mere letter A, as its logical subject, but, instead, means by A "just anything specific.") —Logically valuable identity is asserted of what is not only identical but also distinct. Hegel's logic has the merit of making this clear throughout. Unfortunately that book is not required reading even for Ph.D. candidates in philosophy.

When Medicus says concept and reality are the same, he does not mean the concept of ink is black, nor the concept of lemon sour. Nor can we dip a pen into the first concept, or use the second as a condiment in a green salad. —Some of our self-styled philosophers and logicians are as ignorant of Kant as of Hegel. It was Kant whose very problem of epistemology was to refute the kind of "idealism" which would deny that we can actually know things. In the absence of that philosophical insight, it is no wonder that people came to believe in pragmatism: If it works technically, then it is real and true. Advertising logic is Hitler logic: Just repeat it until it sinks in and customers do not say "aspirin" but "Bayers." Or, more seriously speaking: Just keep saying "communist infiltration" and save yourself the trouble of finding out what is really going on in San Salvador and South America.

Impersonal propositions, though immediately certain, do leave uncertainties. For instance when we feel a first drop of rain we watch for the sensation of a second or we look on the ground for additional wet spots. That is, we already relate the first sensation in more or less explicit thought.

Only the comprehended context grants certainty of existence, and certainty is always selfcertainty. Existence is ascertained in the concept, and of the concept we are certain.

> Obviously Medicus does not use the word concept (Begriff) as a synonym for term or word. Terms are conventional and words are aesthetic creations. But conceptual certainty is selfcertainty. We say: "Oh, I see!"

We can believe in nature and history only because, in nature and in history, we experience ourselves.

> My personal note in brackets says: Of course experience not in the sense of objectivating psychological observation.

My "I" experience is enhanced by every wider comprehension of reality, taken into our selves.

Every mere immediacy brings the task of being comprehended in a concept. Thus the immediate becomes mediated. The essential result of reflection is mediate being. Immediate certainty as yet lacks a context, it is like a point in space, a mere now and here. Reflection does away with that isolation and preserves the purely singular in a general context.

> Medicus uses the one word hebt auf, in the sense which Hegel made so clear, meaning simultaneously "doing away" and "preserving." As far as I know, in English we are coerced to use two terms. That is not altogether bad, because it induces the reader to ask why. His first impression is: paradox! He actually begins to think, which is a good thing, especially in a student. Incidentally the German reader has to think too. Which is why he rarely falls in love with Hegel immediately.

Reflection does not intend to lose the purely singular but rather to know its essence (Wesen).

> The German noun Wesen comes from the root meaning of sein (to be) as we can readily see in our English word was whose aw sound reminds us that the corresponding German war is pronounced long, not short like English what and north-German was.

The essence pertains to singulars in general, not only to one pure singular. Confronted with an unknown, the scholar inquires into its significance or meaning. For instance, for the investigation of X-rays their immediate sensational certainty (a mere optical stimulus) was unessential. The singular is comprehended only in the general or outright universal. From that wider and deeper insight the scholar can then return to the singular which he so comes to own in the concept.

Essence is mediated through reflection which is not immediate but "abstract" and "thought". In the abstract as such the singular has been conquered.

Kantians sometimes believe that one must proceed "from the singular to the general". But the latter is not something far and distinct from the former. It is its essence. The two cannot be torn apart.

For instance the geologist wants to comprehend the Alps, not a mere general planetary shrinking. In geology the singular is irreplaceable. In contrast, physics has no high regard for the singular because it is available everywhere.

June 30 THE LOGIC OF HYPOTHESES AND ERROR

Abstraction is meaningful not because it severs the general from the particular, but because it induces us to inquire into the nature of the particular. We want to grasp the concrete, in a concept of it. Science wants to understand reality.

The now and here is always the starting point. Example: The shorter a tense string, the higher its tone. A playful child can readily observe that. But such playful observation is not yet science. In the "now and here" science seeks a universal validity, starting from the conjecture that there must be some law in the context. Research always starts from the "now and here." And as soon as in what is immediate we seek some relation to a universal validity, we are seeking some knowledge of the essence of what we investigate (Wesenserkenntnis). The sense evidence we have is tentatively fitted into the context of an assumed law. For instance, "gold" is tentatively conceived as "an element." We can think sense evidence only by taking it as a representative of a law. This endeavor is quite different from teaching an animal by having it merely remember whatever we want to teach. Even if the assumed law is not correct, it still endeavors to mediate immediate sense evidence by means of thought.

Are the laws in question supported by "sufficient ground"? Sense evidence as such tells us nothing of law. For instance it yields only the tone of a string. Laws are concerned with essence, which must be thought and is no mere sensuous immediacy. It is reflection that yields the law. However not an indifferently "applied" outward reflection. Rather it is the sense finding itself which is being thought. The sense finding is not-I, which cannot be dissolved in the concept but remains an endless task. Therefore the hypotheses of natural science are not "sufficiently" supported. There always remains a rest which raises new questions. But this endless process is proof of the life of natural science. The questions that occupy us today could not even be raised, were we to stop at the stage of yesterday's science.

This problematic remnant does not cancel out the truth content of the hypothesis. Hypotheses do contain truth because they conform to a necessity of thought which operates already in the formulation of a question, that is, in the endeavor to surmise a law. There are stories about happenstance occurrencies leading to discoveries of natural science. For instance a swinging lamp, a falling apple. [Galilei; Newton.] But such contingent events lack conceptual necessity and can be replaced by other events. The fact that reflection focusses on such contingencies manifests a conceptual necessity which at once liberates the mind from mere contingency, and which furthermore springs from contemporary culture. The questions which determine the character of research have their roots in comprehensive contexts of culture. Very specific problems call for solutions at each particular present time. Science itself stands in a more comprehensive cultural context, as a member seeking that is essential, looking for essence (Wesen).

Great scientists do not unveil any timeless knowledge (by greater intelligence); they join others in carrying the weight of their time whose questions they are capable of formulating. Of course it is possible that cases occur in which a man who lacks cultural width and depth can be confronted by great questions, either by happenstance or else being led to the confrontation by another. Thus our contemporary sculptor Heller once told me (Medicus) that he felt nothing strange in Einstein's feeling for space. I (Medicus) retorted: "I have known that for quite some time, but I did not want to bother you with my knowing it."

I too was acquainted with Heller whom I found a soundly cautious skeptic. (I would not venture to evaluate the width and depth of his historical awareness.) Once I sat in his studio while he was working on a two foot statue of a man bending forward. Of course the wire frame was in the belly part of the little model, not in the place of the spine. Heller had a lump of clay in his left hand and, with his right thumb, pinched off pea size lumps which he then affixed to the kidney section of the statue, while we were chatting. After a while I asked: "Why do you not take lumps the size of a hazelnut or a walnut, instead of going so slowly?" Heller was utterly amazed about my question. He replied: "How could I? If I did I might overshoot the spot where I must stop." Obviously he was building up his statue intuitively and not by means of a kind of mental blue print, like an engineer and mechanic. So skepsis, that is, withholding of rash judgment, was precisely the right procedure. The artist procedes by aesthetic not by conceptual conscience.

Necessity of thought cannot be formulated in timeless concepts. It is an experience in [and of] its time. We cannot experience the theories of Aristotle the way they were an immediate need of truth in their time.

We cultivate the history of natural science because in that history we sense tasks set for our own intellectual life. The hypotheses of natural science are always related to the specific questions of their time, which are always onesided.

July 2

The spirit of culture always demands a selfcertain relation to the time's questions. Whatever is hypothetical is contained in the life of the spirit which itself is not at all hypothetical. Hypotheses are no mere means (Mittel) of this life, a life which is *in* the hypotheses and does not exist without them.

I find it difficult to find the right English word for *Mittel*. The German word *Lebensmittel* means victuals. And any nourishing victual will serve as a means for biological living, though Hindoos may find it awkward to replace rice by wheat. The specific victual does not matter. But in that very sense the hypotheses do matter. The life of the spirit is always specific.

The full meaning of hypotheses is misunderstood if judged only as true or false. Hypotheses that have proved invalid are not on the same level as false news in the newspapers. For these disproven bypotheses have contained the very life of truth which gives them a kind of priestly character indelebilis. The significance of a hypothesis lies in the fact that it endeavors to answer certain difficulties that have become manifest in the history of knowledge. In the life of truth the not-I appears in ever new shape. In the context of the development of science no theory is superfluous, and none is false in its essence. Questions are raised not by a timeless nature but by the stage of development of science. Therefore the answer found by research is not timeless either. In order to understand the theories of the day, we need not necessarily know the history of natural science, yet the theories are the carriers of that history. In the hypotheses themselves there is the urge for further development. The stages of the development are not dead like the rungs of a ladder; they are alive, that is, logical consciousness expresses itself "this and that way." And because they are alive, they themselves are at work to outgrow themselves. A theorem of natural science is nothing rigid as if it were thus once and for all. It is not merely "true or false"; it pushes beyond itself.

The domain of the false is the domain of truth in the making. In seeking sufficient grounds, research did not go far enough. Thus error is too early a stop. In contrast, a hypothesis of natural science is not a stop. The purpose of a theory is not to kill the life of science but to carry it. Galilei tells of an Aristotelian who stuck to the text of Aristotle and to the doctrine that the center of the nervous system is in the heart, not the brain.

The life of science itself will kill its carrier. Anyone who seriously wants to be a scientist should know this. That life explodes its vessels. An hypothesis desires to offer truth, that is, not to be valid only for the specific cases it studied. Thus it demands something greater than itself. Therefore its downfall is not an annihilation from without; it is its own goal, in which its defects are overcome, and its truth is freed. It falls not because of what is false in it. We can call it a dead stop or false, only if we look at its mere formulation. Instead we ought to look for its meaning. The hypothesis dies because it has in itself the life of truth which cannot be retained in any one shape. The hypothesis satisfies the demands already known; yet it ought to grasp the essence of the manifestations studied. That essence is the absolutely universal significance. Concepts are knowledge of essence. To reach a concept means to know the law according to which the manifestation occurs "thus and not otherwise." The contingency of the manifestation (Erscheinung) lies in what is already known historically. But new facts get known which contradict the hypothesis. The concept is to do away with the contingency of the manifestation. However the "sufficient grounds" are never enough.

A hypothesis is always better than its formulation. Yet faced by the available manifestation, the hypothesis does need its specific formulation, no other.

The I is self-certain clearness. The logical I lives in the hypotheses because it knows that new problems will erupt. The I finds a non-finite goal in the contents of thought, by way of distinguishing itself from those contents. In the hypothesis the concepts are restricted by whatever is yet dark and conceptless, for instance the notion of an atom. These dark contents belong to the life of truth which demands that such notions be sacrificed.

Whatever law we assume when we think the given facts is a living unity, a synthetic unity of the manifold [as Kant would say], which claims universal validity. Whether this unity be posited as a judgment or as a concept, be conceptually purified or be a mere current notion, the unity always grasps some manifold and unifies it, for instance the notion a child has of water unifies his sense perceptions of water.

When we think the unity of qualities we call it a substance, and the unity of its changes we call causality.

July 7

> I was in Basel to see Professor Joel. On my return I copied the stenographic notes taken by a fellow student, Goldmann:

SUBSTANCE AND CAUSALITY. THE ATOM

Substance means the unity of a manifold of qualities and accidents. The knowledge of essence (Wesenserkenntnis) also covers the changes that occur in the world. They are conceived under a law. What is so conceived is not merely the sense experience of a change, [as psychology records it]. For the cogency of a law has entered with the concept. Once the occurred change has been so thought we call it a causal event. Substance and causality are the fundamental concepts of physics and of whatever discipline rests on physics like chemistry, mineralogy, etc. — Substance and causality are as inseperable as the now and here of sense certainty, yet also separable in thought like the now and here. In our experience the now and the here are always together. The experience occurs now; the substantial thing is here. However if I have the concept of the substantial unity of certain qualities then I recognize the thing not only where it first confronted me. If I know the substance I recognize it also when it is manifest in different accidents. I have become independent of the mere now and here; I have gained an experiential concept. --If the water turned to ice I still recognize in it the same water I saw before as water. I do not harbor the opinion that somebody poured out the water and put something else in its place. However my recognition of the water rests on the lawfulness of the causal event. Thus we discover that substance and causality belong together. It is my concern with the observed thing that brings me the unity of causality.

We do have the ability to reflect, and in reflection we can separate causality from substance. We can also direct our reflection to the here without the now, and vice versa. We can proceed by abstraction. Thus, in abstraction, we can conceive substance and causality separately. However they cannot be separated in our knowledge of essence (Wesenserkenntnis); there they belong to the thing (Sache).

The temporal state of our knowledge may force us to stop at the mere acknowledgement of a substance without knowing its law. We may have to acknowledge an experience which we can describe without grasping the context of substance and cause. For instance, a physician may acknowledge the precise change in a patient without as yet knowing the cause of the change. He can describe the state of the patient without conceptually understanding the substantial context, which is what he desires to know. Similarly we may be able to describe the progressing change without knowing how this change fits into a substantial context of things. We acknowledge the substance without being able to ascertain their causality. That kind of knowledge lacks the cogency of the concept. Acknowledgment is the boundary of knowledge.

Some people speak of events without causes. An event seems to be without a cause when we are incapable of reaching essential knowledge (Wesenserkenntnis). Of course we know that a knowledge of the cause would mean a progress in our knowing. To know (Erkennen) means to grasp the essence. And we can grasp it only if we do not have to stop at the separate category. We know the essence only when causality and substance fuse. The essence is their unity.

As long as I have merely an abstract knowledge of a chemical element, knowing its atomic weight, etc., the causal relations involved are as yet unknown. Every quality implies causal relationships. Observations like hardness, color, touch, etc., are needed but do not suffice. Our sense observations imply causal changes which occur. The <u>substantial things change</u>; they arise and they vanish. To know their essence requires a knowledge of the causal law of their arising and vanishing.

It is said, <u>substance perseveres</u>, it stands above arising and vanishing. What is this substance over which causality has no power? It is something more than the phenomenal singular thing, the specific conditioned appearance. As the latter changes the substance merely changes its manner of appearing. It changes in line with a law. We may not even know clearly what has become of the thing. The physical observation may be too fragmentary. That makes no difference. We insist. The necessity of thought (die Denknotwendigkeit) forces us to say that what is substantial in the evanescent thing persists.

> <u>Denknotwendigkeit</u> was a favorite word of Medicus. When here he says it forces us he does not mean it robs us of our freedom. In the abstract, of course, "necessity of thought" sounds like a need to scratch, or like a hunger pang, or a sneeze, but as one cannot explain in words the difference between an urge to sneeze and an itch, or hunger, so one cannot tell in the abstract what it means to "have to think". One must experience a specific problem and its "force" that makes one think in specific terms. And this experience is always personal, as Medicus says in his next sentence.

The necessity of thought are we ourselves; it is truth that forces us in its specific way. What is evanescent is called the <u>accidents</u>, that is, the contingent qualities. If I light a piece of paper and let it burn, its appearance changes, its accidents change. But whatever was its substance cannot simply vanish. We even want to measure the persistent substance.

What is this necessary <u>substance</u>? It is a form (Gestalt) of conceptual necessity. <u>The persistent substance is the necessity in which things must be thought</u>. <u>Thinking</u> is nothing merely subjective; it is the self-knowledge of the contents of thought. Necessity of thought lies in the contents of thought.

Again, such a sentence means nothing in the abstract. Only a specific thought has necessity. And to philosophize means to remind oneself of this simple fact. In the introduction to his lectures on the history of philosophy (XIII, 37) Hegel says "it is an ordinary prejudice that philosophy deals only with abstractions, with empty generalities", but "philosophy is most inimical to the abstract; it leads back to the concrete." In his lectures on the philosophy of religion Hegel says "it is the cowardice of abstract thought to shun what is present to the senses, in a monkish manner; modern abstraction habitually puts on such fastidious airs confronted by sense presence" (Glockner ed. 16:309). And in the Logic of the Encyclopedia Hegel says: "He who is too fastidious with regard to the finite never attains any reality but remains in the abstract and [like a dying candle] burns out in himself" (92 Zusatz, VI, 182). Hegel also speaks of the dead skull, "the caput mortuum of abstraction" (ib., Glockner ed. 8:262). --I am quoting all these passages from Hegel because they underline the main concern of the "concrete logic" of Medicus.

Substance is an aspect (Moment) of the essence of natural things, of things as objects of physical knowledge. The knowledge of physical essence is a necessary aspect (Gestalt) of the truth of life (Lebenswahrheit). However we can grasp the essence only by thinking. When natural science seeks knowledge, it can have no other purpose than the formulation of the necessity of thinking.

What we comprehend as this necessity of persistent substance are not the natural things (die Naturdinge).

One feels the things as now and here. Therefore the things become again something accidental. Therewith arises the task to comprehend this as a necessary being. What must be done is to trace the substantial individual things back to the necessary unchangeable substance.

Thus the opinion arises that one will meet the persistent essence of things if one goes back to the smallest particles (die kleinsten Teilchen) of the natural things. Natural science dissects things into molecules and these are further dissected into elements, compounds and atoms. The path that leads from ordinary sense thinking to the atom is the causal process. Mechanical dissection and chemical analysis (Auflösung). Thus it becomes obvious (es versteht sich) that the final phase (Endinstanz) even of the atoms can be nothing else than the ordinary . . .

> HM Goldmann's notes which Marti copied have gaps. How much of the physics which Goldmann reports and which was already outdated in 1919 goes on his account, and how much on that of Medicus is not clear. Medicus was probably strongly influenced by L. Poincaré's book "Moderne Physik", a German translation from the French published by Quelle und Meyer at Leipzig in 1908. This book was written for philosophically interested readers. One should remember that Rutherford postulated his atomic model (a small nucleus surrounded by electrons) in 1911, based on his famous scattering experiments with alpha particles. Niels Bohr, in 1913, went one step further, connecting Planck's and Einstein's quantum theory with Rutherford's model. There were still inherent difficulties connected with this planetary model, and a minority of physicists and other scientists were not yet convinced about the new atomic theory. Only in 1923, after the experiments on the scattering of X rays by A.H. Compton, the evidence for the atomic theory was so overwhelming that it was generally accepted.

Even the smallest particles are substantial. The atoms need not have sense qualities, as the thing (die Sache) from which we started. Just as the rays can be ascertained by an indirect way, a similar indirect observation of atoms may turn out to be possible.

> HM The rays that can be ascertained by an indirect way are probably the X rays, which one cannot see directly. One only sees the light produced by them on a fluorescent screen, or one sees the blackening of a photographic plate.

Only by reflection can one attribute to the atoms the property of . . . [gap]. Therefore it is no immediate sensuous certainty that leads to the certainty of the qualities which the substantial things would have to have.

Substantiality and causality are not to be separated. And if the smallest particles of reality can surely (doch) be found by the way of causal processes, it is obvious (versteht sich) that these substantial individual things, just like other substantial individual things, are inseparable of the causal process.

An atomistic explanation of the world (des Weltalls) is the goal toward which physics is working with undeniable success. This shows more and more clearly that electrical atoms are the last units to which everything (alles Seiende) is to be reduced; the last building stone. However the justification of these results is historically conditioned. That is, the atomistic conception has grown from the task that confronts the physics of our days. The physics of the present time has the task to pursue the path thus opened (diesen angebahnten Weg) toward the reduction to electrical atoms.

> HM The expression "electrical atom" is found in Poincaré's book, p. 72: "as the newest theories represent the atoms as centers that consist of atoms of electricity." When Poincaré wrote this, one knew that electrons are constituents of the atoms, but that they had very little mass. At that time it was in no way clear with which constituents the bulk of the mass and the compensating positive charge were associated. James Jeans wrote in his book "The Growth of Physical Science" (Cambridge, 1951) p. 306, describing the situation from 1906 on: "To the question 'What is the ultimate substance of the Universe?' which had puzzled science from the time of Thales on, it at last seems possible to give an answer--the one word 'electricity'."

Surely, on the way of such reduction, valuable insights are to be gained. However we are dealing only with an hypothesis. The task is to get around some very specific difficulties which have come forward. The physicist of today is not at all concerned with what he will have to think once he is beyond the goal desired today. He is not thinking up possibilities and tasks of physics in the 22nd century. Nothing would come of that kind of thinking. Something can come of such "thinking beyond" (Weiterdenken) only if, in the steady historical movement of physics the very goal of today has already begun to become problematical. The present goal of electrical atomistic will lead into new crises. Then the time will have come when the present goal of physics will have been displaced by other formulations of physical science. For, as long as the electrical atoms can pass for ultimate units, they are as yet hardly known at all; as yet they are the limit (Grenze) of our knowledge. What I know is only this variable limit which is being pushed further and further out. These atoms merely seem to be without causality (kausalitätslos), but they really are not. The atoms, as so far accepted, become the object or topic (Gegenstände) of knowledge; they are to be absorbed in the causal context.

Fifty years ago the chemical atoms seemed without causality. They were rigid building stones. Then came the new physics. The atoms were no longer the last units. No longer are they merely acknowledged, but they are known, being known as causal things. Causality and substantiality lead into being (ins Sein).

One has found out the essence of the atoms. The same spectacle is beginning with regard to the electrical atoms of our time. They too will become objects of knowledge. The things which happen to lie on the frontier of our knowing are what one must merely acknowledge (was man bloß anerkennen kann), and as long as that substance and causality seem to be apart. As soon as the things are known, substance and causality are together as a unit.

July 9 TIME AND SPACE. MATHEMATICS

Molecules and atoms are objects which inseparably carry in themselves their causality. The way to them will not some day stop at the "smallest". They are substantial individual things (Einzeldinge) which are causally conditioned. Where is the "last perseverant" (das letzte Beharrliche)?

The ultimate necessity of thinking does away with the abstract isolation of the substantial thing (abstrakte Vereinzelung des substantiellen Dings). It shows that the perseverant substance is present in all things. To think the perseverant substance means to think what conditions all things (was alle Dinge bedingt--what thingifies all things); it is not imaginable (vorstellbar) but only thinkable. One tries to imagine it (to set it up in front of oneself) as an atom; however that is not possible. To think the perseverant substance means to think at the same time causality which is its own unity. The law (Gesetzmäßigkeit) in the change (im Anderswerden) of all things is the perseverant substance. The essence of water does not evaporate; it perseveres precisely in the fact that steam is exactly determined. In the same sense of law of nature, energy of movement is transformed into energy of heat; the law perseveres.

Analysis unifies; it demonstrates the same original objects (Urobjekte) and laws in all natural events. The goal is to reduce all natural events to the same ultimate essences. This goal is necessary and also impossible, because only an absolutely unchangeable and ultimate could be perseverant substance. Yet an abstract substance separated from causality is useless in natural science. The Not-I cannot be ultimately dissolved in and for the life of truth. Ultimate units would be the death of science. "Ultimate concepts" in explanatory natural science are nothing fixed; they are historically conditioned hypotheses.

The now and here is vanquished (überwunden) by the concept of substance and causality. These laws of reflective thinking overcome (überwinden) by the concept of substance and causality. These laws of reflective thinking overcome (überwinden) those limitations. In the immediacy of sense certainty there is no separate space and time, but only an as yet incomprehended (unbegriffenes) given (Gegebenes). In real thought, space and time are one; only in reflection are they separated.

Our walking foot dodges the stone without inquiring into its essence. Sense certainty is incomprehended reality; for instance, this wall is at first glance only a limit posited as a limit in our sense perception. Then our consciousness makes clear that the wall has a back side, not only the sensuously perceived front. Consciousness, as it were, penetrates the wall. Our consciousness of space contains the wall. Sense certainty limits. The concept comprehends the wall as substantial thing, located in space and time. Thus I know more although I no longer merely see. --Another example: The sound of a hitting axe is quite separate in sense perception from the sight of the axe hitting. Then reflection posits the two perceptions in time, by thinking of the causality of light waves and sound waves. Thus my time consciousness is no longer merely immediate, and no longer limited by incomprehension. Owing to the togetherness of substance and causality our consciousness of space and time pervades everything, without limit (ins Unendliche). The *conceptual* necessity of causality pervades time by showing that, at *all* times, it is valid (erfüllt). Fichte said the thinking of reflection is a spatial and temporal "drawing of lines."

The *comprehending I* does not let itself be limited absolutely by the *Not-I*. The vanquishing (Aufhebung) of the limitation cannot be separated from the knowledge of essence, by means of causality and substantiality. If I knew what the thing is essentially (eigentlich), I would know *how* it is in space. The *Not-I* is an infinite task but not an *absolute* limit; in *principle* it is always solvable.

Space and time are infinitely divisible only in reflection; in *immediate sense* certainty they are unconditionally indivisible.

Münsterberg, psychologist at Harvard University, says our experience of time (Zeiterleben) of two seconds is not twice one second. Only in reflection do we think of the thousand millimeters in a meter, and of all the spectral colors in white light. Of course such reflection is legitimate. But it is not an immediate sense perception.

No mathematical shape (Gebilde) is the object of sense perception (Anschauung). Pure extension is only in reflection. The mathematical space is not logically prior to the real space. Only by reflection do we come from the physical space to the mathematical.

July 14

Pure extension as connection (Gemeinsames) of time and space is significant for knowledge by the fact that by this connection the now and here are actively interpenetrated (tätig durchdrungen). Only by being filled with causality is time a function of knowledge, and so is space owing to the thing (Gegenstand) in it. Geometry is pure extension as spatial. Arithmetic is yet antecedent (oberhalb) to the space-time distinction; for numbers apply to a line as well as to time. What is immediately experienced (erlebt) in space and time is not divisible; along with divisibility (in reflection) comes also countability. In every point of a line the I is certain of itself. Reflection vanquishes (überwindet) the now and here. The stuff of mathematics is the product of reflection; therefore the mathematical forms (Gebilde) have an abstract existence. They are logically later than concrete existence. The concrete object (Gegenstand) is a synthetic unity of a manifold whose individual qualities (e.g. hardness, color) however are independent of each other. No quality contributes to the imaginability (Vorstellbarkeit) of another. Mathematical forms (Gebilde) are of pure extension; consequently their individual qualities are not independent of each other. For instance "3" is three indistinguished unities. If the concrete object is divested of all concreteness there remains an entirely abstract unity; for instance, out of "sweet, hard, white" we get only "three". Geometric forms are somewhat more concrete than arithmetical ones. The latter are divested of all concreteness.

In the case of geometric forms we can still make further abstractions by means of arithmetic presentations. The geometric forms have a relation to space though they are not space. The relation to the space of concrete reality which is a metric field is itself a problem. The matter which is manifest in space (den Raum durchwirkend) is what gives that space its specific qualities. Our concrete consciousness of space implies an obscure acknowledgment of its metric determination. The ascertainment of the metric structure of space is a vast task and ultimately remains as hypothetical as every other physical knowledge. Pure extension stands to concrete space as the I to the Not-I. Abstracting geometry arbitrarily gives its spaces their axioms. Therefore the geometric forms pertain entirely to the sphere of abstract reflection. Therefore they lack an essential, concrete synthetical unity. Thus, for instance, "white" can be represented (vorgestellt) without the other qualities of sugar, but the equilateralness cannot be presented without the other qualities of the triangel.

THE LOWEST DEGREE OF EXISTENCE

The lowest degree of existence is still a step below: Every existential judgment simply asserts a higher degree of existence than the one presupposed as a matter of course (der selbstverständlich vorausgesetzte). The latter is manifest in negative judgments regarding existence. For instance, "there is a plain triangle" but "there is no plain two-angle;" it is impossible to construct such a form; that is quite insoluble. An affirmative judgment signifies solubility. For instance "there are irrational numbers." The solution places the now concrete concept into its (here mathematical) context. Specific qualities are postulated and are to form a synthetic unity. Therefore mathematical problems lie in the sphere of indefinite relations of magnitudes. The selfcertainty of this sphere is required for the solution. Of the law of the sphere we are certain: It is pure extension whose creator is the I insofar as the I overcomes the sense-image limitation (die sinnlich-anschauliche Begrenztheit). Like Adam to Eve: "This is bone of my bone."

Without a Not-I there would be no I. The objective world is never fully known without remainder, because totality would require an infinitely sufficient substantiation (Begründung). Reflection comprehends something limited, only finite objects. Thus pure extension is inevitably cut into pieces; and thus a "straight line" is comprehensible only as "the shortest line between two points", yet that presupposes the infinity of the straight line.

> This may need a more explicit mathematical presentation.

From this contrast between the infinity of the life of truth and the limitation of reflection spring the problems of mathematical axioms.

Substance and causality demand ultimate unity which, however, is set aside (aufgehoben) again by the further process of research. Physical categories [seem to be] self-identical building stones (e.g. substance) and rigid laws; still they can be overcome (überwunden) only hypothetically.

BIOLOGICAL SCIENCES

As mathematics stand to physics, so seems anatomy (in the widest sense) to stand to whatever is alive. However physics tries to comprehend change (das Anderswerden) in terms of rigid self-identity, while alive identity is not rigidly identical with itself. Accommodation or adjustment (Anpassung) is its fundamental concept. Precisely in order to assert itself as alive, the living (be it individual or species) adapts itself to the environment and thus changes. And this occurs in strictest connection with nourishment; a living identity builds itself from foreign material (Stoff).

Thinking is life that knows itself. On that account, thinking is the key to the fact of organic life. The interpenetration of egg cell and sperm cell can be objectively described but not understood as objective. However when, in no mere outward manner, a subject and a predicate are joined and thus find their togetherness in a new insight, therein lies the "secret" of the organic. (You will have to think of some important insight into the relationship of a perhaps almost dead subject and predicate.)

> I wonder why Medicus did not himself give an example. If he had, I would surely have made a note, especially of this so very important matter of the "secret of the organic."
>
> The reader will wonder how the model of a purely intellectual togetherness, like that of a logical subject with its predicate, can apply at all to the riddle of a unifying biological togetherness of a sperm with an ovum. Does one not simply beg the question of organic life, if one predicates intentionality of sperms and ova, or predicates even as little as a subconscious satisfaction of having died in each other and thus become one? --I am not attributing to Medicus such notions as these. I merely want to ask what kind of bio-logical thinking would have to be developed to establish a comparable parallel between thinking biological events and thinking the coming together of logical subject and predicate. I have no answer.

As for the "coming together", in Latin literally convenientia, I cannot help remembering Augustine's "con-venience" of "the interior man with his inhabitor", that is, with the living truth. I will quote and also translate the passage in *de vera religione* (xxxix, 72):

Quaere in corporis voluptate quid teneat, nihil aliud invenies quam convenientiam: nam si resistentia pariant dolores, convenientia pariunt voluptatem. Recognosce igitur quae sit summa convenientia. Noli foras ire; in te ipsum redi; in interiore homine habitat veritas: et si tuam naturam mutabilem inveneris, transcende et teipsum: Sed memento cum te transcendis, ratiocinantem animam te transcendere. Illuc ergo tende, unde ipsum lumen rationis accenditur. Quo enim pervenit omnis bonus ratiocinator, nisi ad veritatem? cum ad seipsam veritas non utique ratiocinando perveniat, sed quod ratiocinantes appetunt, ipsa sit. Vide ibi convenientiam qua superior esse non possit; et ipse conveni cum ea. Confitere te non esse quod ipsa est: siquidem seipsa non quaerit: tu autem ad ipsam quaerendo venisti, non locorum spatio, sed mentis affectu, ut ipse interior homo cum suo inhabitatore, non infima et carnali, sed summa et spirituali voluptate conveniat.

"If you ask what charms us in bodily pleasure, you find nothing else than togetherness (or convenience in the literal Latin sense). While resistances give birth to pain, conveniences bear pleasure. Therefore recognize what is highest togetherness. Do not go outside. Go back into your self. Truth dwells in the inner man. And if you find your nature mutable, go deeper than yourself. But remember that, in thus transcending yourself, you are transcending the ratiocinating soul. Therefore tend toward the [point] whence the light of reason itself is lit. For where does the good reasoner arrive if not at the truth? Yet truth does not at all arrive at itself by ratiocination, because it *is* what the ratiocinators desire. Behold, there is a togetherness higher than which there is none. And do come together with it yourself. Admit that you are not what the truth itself is. For truth does not seek itself, but you came to it by seeking, not in spatial locations but by a state of mind, so that the interior man himself comes together with his inhabitor, not in a low and carnal, but in the

> highest and spiritual pleasure."
> The insight that consists in this fusion with truth which is "our highest teacher, teaching inwardly" (de libero arbitrio II, ii, 4) is here the "key" to understanding what is organic.

Formal logic looks at our thinking as if it were something objective and therefore foreign. But the alive essence (das lebendige Wesen), the becoming one of subject and predicate, demands to be lived. Organic existence is immediate; it is no mere objective existence like the mathematical-physical. Knowledge of what is alive seeks empathy (Miterleben) with what is not merely foreign.

July 16

Biological sciences deal with what is not merely objective, but with immediate existence, with living "substance" and living causality. Not very much can be done with causal equations although, of course, the chemical and physical laws are not invalid. But they yield only an abstract knowledge. In contrast, any specific thought develops like a plant, differing in line with soil and conditions. Thus a thought pertaining to science can be distinguished from the same thought as it is manifest in different heads, just as the species can be distinguished from its manifestation in individuals. Likewise, thoughts have their evolutionary history. The essential identity remains: life is here and there. However there is another distinction [between thoughts and plants]: the individual species of plants is not as important for biology as plant life as such [while specific thoughts are more important in logic than thinking in general]. (The general is all the more important in the physical sciences.) Thus the path of natural science leads to the abstract, to the most general laws. A knowledge of a dozen plants already affords some insight into the world of plants, but the knowledge of several single thoughts furnishes at best a few logical examples. Scientific [that is systematic] thoughts however are more than examples; they claim a significance of their own; they refuse to serve as samples in [abstract] logic. To be sure there is a similar relationship of the single plant to botany. However the knowledge of the single plant only serves botany, whereas the single scientific thought claims its own significance (sich selbst will).

In organic nature the immediate life is still deeply tied in objectivity(ins Gengenständliche hineingebunden), and the objectively real yields only to an abstract conceptuality.

> This sounds cryptic. The word, das Gegenständliche, must be taken quite literally: der Gegenstand steht mir entgegen. Medicus was fond of quoting Jacob Boehme's translation of obiectum as quite literally Gegenwurf. The object (as the Latin word says) is "thrown at me." And it offers resistance, Widerstand, to the effort at knowing it. In this sense, I believe, Medicus here says that, although the organic is alive, yet it is still object. As physicists and engineers we learn how to manage physical objects, by means of mathematical abstractions.
> But confronted with organisms the more we abstract the less we know of the life of the organism. That was the theme of Schelling's Naturphilosophie. But what can empathy accomplish by way of knowledge?

HISTORICAL DISCIPLINES

Reality (die Wirklichkeit) [welche wirkt], is still more than the biological whose truth value is not unconditional.

> But the immediate so und nicht anders (thus, and no other way) of a poem is unconditional. And at the other end, so is the immediate insight into mathematical truth. --Faced with health books, I cussedly reply: "I can taste what is good and healthy for me!" But I do not call it science.

It would be as much a mistake to make physics or biology an autocrat (Alleinherrscherin) as to cling to the mere existential judgment es blitzt, there is lightning, and thus not to go beyond the now and here. If we widen the domain of biology unconditionally, we thereby cover up the peculiar significance (den Eigenwert) of a higher life under a [biological] abstraction. To grasp that higher life is the task of the historical disciplines (Wissenschaften). Thus, for instance, psychiatric findings do not furnish historical insights. True, the historian will take them into account like other natural facts. Like the other sciences historiography does not stop at facts; it does not consist of a sum of informations (Einzelerkenntnis). However, unlike the natural sciences, historiography does not place the single event in an abstract law. The singular has its own value because historiography deals with a free life that stands above nature. Freedom posits itself as reality. This life makes itself responsible; it does not stop; it always pushes on, beyond itself. (The "state" of the bees remains what it is and can be described in the abstract.) Historical changes are not phenomena of adaptation. The autonomously responsible life always finds a reason (Grund) to go beyond itself; the spirit of culture is never satisfied even for a moment. It is responsible to itself, for it is the immediate selfcertainty of truth which always seeks for its sufficient ground. For this very reason every standpoint once reached must be overcome. It is the moral demand that we treat reality as what it is in truth.

The life of our time, which comprehends (umfasst) past and future presents itself in art, while science (Wissenschaft; here: historiography) endeavors to understand finite forms (Gestalten). In history we do not seek abstract generalities. To be sure we seek the proper place for the single [fact or event], but we seek it in the life of cultural communities, in which the singular retains its own value. The historian shapes the fullness of singularities into the unity of a non-arbitrary cultural image (Kulturbild). The "historical art" (Schelling's phrase) remains faithful to reality, though the facts may be few, like the details of a picture.

INDEX

INDEX OF NAMES

INDEX OF TOPICS

Bibliography

Books by Medicus:

1905 J.G. Fichte. Dreizehn Vorlesungen.
1917 Grundfragen der Aesthetik.
1922 Fichtes Leben. Zweite, umgearbeitete Auflage.
1926 Die Freiheit des Willens und ihre Grenzen.
1927 Pestalozzis Leben.
1943 Vom Wahren, Guten und Schönen.
1944 Das Mythologische in der Religion.
1951 Menschlichkeit. Die Wahrheit als Erlebnis und Verwirklichung.
1954 Vom Überzeitlichen in der Zeit. Beiträge zur humanistischen Besinnung.

Medicus first made himself known as the editor of the works of Fichte (1908-10) and as his biographer (1905, 1914) introducing those works.--He wrote uncounted numbers of contributions to journals, periodicals and collections of essays. He was a regular contributor to the cultural section of the leading Swiss daily, the Neue Zürcher Zeitung. The totality of these writings may be as important as his books. At least one of these essays ought to be mentioned; it locates the place of philosophy among the scholarly disciplines and marks philosophy's relation to faith. It is one of six lectures delivered by representatives of different disciplines, October 9th and 10th, 1943 at the University of Zürich, and published in the volume Wissenschaft und Glaube (Zürich, Eugen Rentsch Verlag). Its title is simply "Philosophie", pages 112-134.

Available in English

1936 "On the Objectivity of Historical Knowledge." Translated by George Brown, University of Glasgow. Pages 137-158 of Philosophy and History. Essays presented to Ernst Cassirer. Edited by Raymond Klibansky. (Oxford, Clarendon Press).

1968 For the International Congress for Philosophy held in September at Vienna (Austria) I wrote a mosaic of quotations from the later works of Medicus, entitled "Versuch einer Würdigung des Werkes". It is available in my Collected Papers on Religion and Philosophy (Washington, University Press of America, 1979, pages 103-112 followed by my translation on pages 113-124).

1973 On Being Human. My translation of Medicus' Menschlichkeit. (New York 1973; now available with a literary appendix, at Warren H. Green, Publisher, 8356 Olive Blvd., St. Louis, Missouri 63132).

BIOGRAPHIC NOTES

Fritz Medicus was born April 23, 1876 as the son of a pharmacist in Stadtlauringen, a small town in Franconia, the northern part of Bavaria. After a classical highschool education including Latin, Greek, and Hebrew, he became first a student of theology, but shifted to philosophy. He attended the universities of Jena, Kiel, and Strassburg, and in 1898 obtained his doctor's degree from the university of Jena with a thesis on Kant's transcendental esthetics and the non-Euclidian geometry. In 1901, he became a Privatdozent--approximately equivalent to an unpaid lecturer--at the University of Halle. He also was secretary to the editor of the "Kant-Studien", the philosopher Hans Vaihinger. In 1911, he accepted the chair of philosophy and pedagogics at the Swiss Federal Institute of Technology in Aürich, which he occupied until his retirement in 1946. The division of humanities and social studies of this school did not grant academic degrees, but every student of the Institute had to register each semester for at least one course in that division. Most of these were pure lecture courses, without reading assignments, homework, or examinations. Even attendance was very much optional. In the nineteenhundredtens and twenties the lectures of Medicus were very popular, and at times it was difficult to find a free seat in the auditorium. Not only the students of the Institute, but also those of the neighboring University of Zürich (including philosophy majors), colleagues of Medicus, and outsiders came to his lectures. His position at the Institute did not permit him to have his own philosophy students; on the other hand, he profoundly influenced the thinking of many future engineers and scientists. Nevertheless, Medicus considered two philosophers his pupils, Paul Tillich from his years in Halle, and Fritz Marti. HM

Medicus died January 13, 1956. Not long before he had been elected to the italian Accademia Nazionale dei Lincei. FM

Heinrich A. Medicus, a son of Fritz Medicus, was born in Zürich in 1918. He studied physics at the Swiss Federal Institute of Technology in Zürich, earning his doctorate in 1949. In 1950, he immigrated to the United States. He is presently a professor of physics at the Rensselaer Polytechnic Institute in Troy, N.Y. His research interests are in experimental nuclear physics and history of modern physics.

Fritz Marti was born in Winterthur, in 1894. 1915-18 he studied mechanical engineering at the ETH. He made his doctorate in philosophy at the University of Bern in 1922. From 1923 to 1973 he taught at a dozen colleges and universities in the USA. He is Emeritus Professor of Philosophy at Southern Illinois University in Edwardsville. His main interests are Schelling, Augustine and philosophy of religion.